Pagan Portals
Sulis

Solar Goddess of the Spring Waters

Pagan Portals
Sulis

Solar Goddess of the Spring Waters

Rachel Patterson

MOON BOOKS

London, UK
Washington, DC, USA

CollectiveInk

First published by Moon Books, 2024
Moon Books is an imprint of Collective Ink Ltd.,
Unit 11, Shepperton House, 89 Shepperton Road, London, N1 3DF
office@collectiveinkbooks.com
www.collectiveinkbooks.com
www.moon-books.net

For distributor details and how to order please visit the 'Ordering' section on our website.

Text copyright: Rachel Patterson 2023

ISBN: 978 1 80341 026 5
978 1 80341 027 2 (ebook)
Library of Congress Control Number: 2023944730

A CIP catalogue record for this book is available from the British Library.

Design: Lapiz Digital Services

UK: Printed and bound by CPI Group (UK) Ltd, Croydon, CR0 4YY
Printed in North America by CPI GPS partners

We operate a distinctive and ethical publishing philosophy in all areas of our business, from our global network of authors to production and worldwide distribution.

CONTENTS

Part II – Working with Sulis

Introduction

Sulis, solar goddess of the hot spring
Hear me now as I invite you in
Power, energy and strength of the sun
I honour you now, as this vow is done

Sulis is one of the very ancient English goddesses, from evidence found we know that she was worshipped at the hot springs in Bath, in the UK, going back to at least the Mesolithic period. Sadly, there are no myths or legends about her, and ancient Britons did not write anything down. What we know about her can only be deemed from the archaeological finds at the Roman Baths in Bath in Somerset and a few mentions in ancient Roman documents. What I do know is that she must have been extremely powerful, and her presence continues to carry that energy forward. I have included within this book, information about the Roman Baths because that sets the scene. The historical information is drawn from archaeological finds and academic viewpoints from experts in their field. Little or nothing is known or has been found about the goddess herself, or how she was honoured. I ask that you allow me a little leeway here, as I have included my own personal gnosis for that part of the book. Hopefully it will give you an introduction to connect with Sulis yourself and discover and create your own relationship with her.

Sulis and Me

My journey with Sulis began a number of years ago, in fact it was in July of 2009 when my husband and I paid a visit to the beautiful city of Bath for a short break. I had heard about the Roman Baths but did not know much about them. We were lucky enough to visit the Baths one evening during our visit. In the summer months they open later, and the main bath is lit by flaming torches. It is a wonderfully haunting and atmospheric experience. It was during this visit that Sulis caught my attention and has held it ever since. Since that first visit, we have been back to Bath on several occasions as a couple, with family, and me and the Kitchen Witch Coven team. On each occasion we make a point of going to see the baths, walking around them and taking in the energy and information. All the exhibits are well marked and give detailed information, you can also listen to one of those funky digital talking gizmos as you walk around too. It is incredibly well laid out and set up for you to make the most of it. If you ever get the chance to visit the Roman Baths, I encourage you to do so, it has a fascinating energy. In fact, if you ever get to visit the city of Bath, I would also encourage you to do so, it is a beautiful place with plenty to see and do.

On my first visit, Sulis made herself known but only in a subtle 'I am a goddess, find out more about me' kind of way. From that point I began my research, and that research has continued, but sadly there is not a huge amount of information out there on her. I have read books by archaeologists who have worked on the baths (I highly recommend anything by Barry Cunliffe), one or two books that mention her in passing and as many academic papers as I could get my hands on. But the information is very sparse. I have listed my recommendations at the end of this book. The information included within this book about the Roman Baths is to help set the scene and has been taken from archaeological finds and those that are experts in their field. The information on Sulis, her characteristics and how to connect with her are for the most part based on my own personal interactions and my journey with her, because there is not much historical evidence or information. Hopefully it will guide you to begin your own journey with her.

Sulis has appeared in two of our online courses we have run as Kitchen Witch, our Celtic Goddess course (now only available to students at our Kitchen Witch online School) and our Goddesses of Ancient Britain online course. We also held an open ritual dedicated to her in June of 2014. I do see her name cropping up on social media occasionally now, so she is no longer forgotten as she once was and her energy is building, putting her out there in the mainstream Pagan world.

Note: When researching for this book I did an internet search for 'Goddess Sulis'. It was an interesting, horrifying and bemusing experience. The few websites that did mention Sulis gave a list of correspondences for her, most of them completely random, but with no references or sources giving reasons for the connections. Sadly, a lot of them were just copied and pasted from other sites. The information given on a lot of the sites was given as fact. There is literally nothing historically recorded about this goddess, where on earth did all this information come from? It was a reminder that not everything you read is correct and there is a lot of misinformation and basic absolute tosh out there. Research, research, research and double check the sources, always.

An Anecdote

In September 2021 myself, Ness, Heather and Sue (the Kitchen Witch posse) went on a pilgrimage to Bath. Obviously, it was not my first visit, but it was for the girls. One of the first stops we made was to the Roman Baths. As we walked from our accommodation, approaching the baths from the back of them, Heather suddenly stopped in her tracks. She felt the energy of Sulis before we had even reached the front of the building. We all stood with her and opened up our spidey senses and yep sure enough there she was. And the goddess Sulis was not happy, oh boy was she not happy. Heather picked up on it first and we all agreed – Sulis was incredibly angry that the cathedral had been built over her temple and how domineering it was, overshadowing the main open bath.

Forward onto our actual visit and we all spent a long time within the walls of the Roman Baths, particularly sitting on the steps gazing up at the temple pediment that show cases the 'gorgon's head' (or Belenus as I prefer to think of it).

After our visit we headed to the cathedral, which is right next door and a gorgeous building, albeit very imposing as it does look over the edge of the baths like some kind of spectre.

We all entered the cathedral at the same time but wandered off on our own explorations. Ness likes to search old churches for signs of the green man! None of us were in there for very long and we all met up again outside a short while afterwards. We all looked at each other and realised we had all felt the same. None of us were meant to be in there, none of us liked the energy, we all wanted to get out of there as quickly as we could. That is not any reflection on the cathedral itself which is a stunning building, we have all visited many ancient churches and the like before. But Sulis did not want us to be in there and we each of us got the message pretty quickly. She is definitely feisty when she wants to be (which in my experience is most of the time).

PART I

Sulis, the history

To Begin With

The best place to start our journey is at the Roman Baths in the beautiful city of Bath in Somerset, England. The reason for starting here is because this is the hub of our story, evidence or mention of the goddess Sulis has only ever been found in Bath.

Today a wonderful sand coloured stone set of buildings stand over the natural hot springs that emerge from beneath the ground. They were put in place by the Romans who loved a good hot spa to bathe in, but archaeological evidence tells us that the goddess Sulis was worshipped at this place long before the Romans arrived. Before the Romans, the site would have just been a natural spring set in nature. We believe ancient Britons would have worshipped outside in nature, they would not have had buildings or temples. Possibly their spiritual rituals would have taken place within groves of trees.

One of the interesting points of note is that Bath does not seem to have been a major Roman city, it was not an important part of the Roman empire nor was it a military base. It was on the far reaches of any of the major Provinces. Despite this, the Romans built huge elaborate structures over the natural springs and kept them beautifully maintained over a long period of time. It would appear that the temple and baths at Bath were seen as a religious place for worship.

Author Bob Stewart writes:

> *The importance of the place, to Roman and non-Roman alike, was rooted in the hot springs. The central elements of the site are the springs, the temple and the baths, dedicated to the goddess Sulis, with various other deities or powers attached and loosely related in the typical Pagan manner. The design of the building with the Gordon's head upon its pediment was typical of a native worship site under strong classical influence' its Greek and Roman*

style combined with Celtic symbolism suggest that it may be a replacement or addition to an existing worship site.[1]

Once the Romans discovered the natural hot springs and that the locals worshipped the goddess Sulis there, they adopted her as their own, although they aligned her with one of their Roman goddesses, Minerva. Adding their own deities with local ones was a regular practice for the Romans.

There are other historical mentions of Bath such as this one from Gaius Julius Solinus, a 3rd century Roman geographer in his book about the wonders of the world. This paragraph seems to have been written about Britain in general but could only be about the hot springs in Bath.

The circumference of Britain is 4875 miles. In this space are many great rivers, and hot springs refined with opulent splendour for the use of mortal men. Minerva is the patroness of these springs. In her shrine, the perpetual fires never whiten into ashes. When they dwindle away, they change into stony globules.[2]

And this quote from an early 9th Century writing, *Historia Brittonum*:

The third wonder is the Hot Lake, where the Baths of Badon are. (..) It is surrounded by a wall, made of brick and stone, and men may go there to bathe at any time, and every man can have the kind of bath he likes. If he wants, it will be a cold bath; and if he wants a hot bath, it will be hot.[3]

Worship at the Springs Is Ancient

In 1998 a small borehole was drilled into the sediment of the hot bath spring and a collection of 494 stone tools that date back to the early Mesolithic period were found. That makes them about 9500 years old. Just this small borehole produced so many items, the experts estimate there may be 1700 artefacts per cubic metre sitting in the muds of the spring.[4] The tools look to be relatively unused leading to speculation they were offerings made to the spirit or goddess of the natural spring.

This was a time of hunter gatherers, pre-farming and just beginning to colonise Britain. The hot springs must have been a surprising find for them, they probably would not have ever experienced anything like it before. The steam and heat from the waters, the slight metallic smell and the orange and green algae that grows around the hot waters would have seemed very magical. Then the sight of three pools of hot water bubbling and steaming away. We do not know much, if anything about the spiritual beliefs of Mesolithic man but I suspect they were either fearful or in awe of this phenomenon or perhaps a little of both.

More archaeological finds show that this spot was visited regularly in the period afterwards up to 5000 or 6000 years ago. When farmers settled in the surrounding area the springs it seems were left pretty much alone. Perhaps people feared them, or they may have been treated as a sacred site that only a dedicated priest was allowed to visit.

The Springs

The springs themselves are thought to be around 12000 years old, from the end of the last ice age. Rain falls onto the limestone in the Mendip hills and from rocks to the north and west, it soaks in and flows in the beds that run from there under the clay and mudstone of the hillsides and valleys. The thousands of feet of rock press down on it from above, heating it and then it rises under Bath, breaking through into a low-lying river bend. Although we understand some of the science behind it no one seems to understand why the three hot springs appear here and nowhere else.

The three springs pump 1.44 million litres (over 300,000 gallons) of water to the surface every 24 hours. The temperature varies slightly but is between 44-46C (111-115F). These are the only true hot springs in the British Isles.

The springs are not just thermal, they are also mineral containing at least 38 minerals including calcium, sodium, potassium, magnesium, hydrogen carbonate and chlorine. It was perhaps these minerals that gave the spring its reputation for being healing waters.

Roll on to the early first century AD and a causeway of gravel and mud was placed into the main spring pool. This would have allowed people to walk out into the centre of the main pool. This may have served as an entry way where they could then make offerings into the waters. A lot of the offerings seem to have been in the form of coins. Seventeen coins from the local British tribe the Dobunni were found in a dig in 1979. A few remnants of pre-Roman pottery have also been recovered close to the springs. But no one built on the area of the springs until the Romans.

In 43 AD the Roman army invaded Britain, and in less than two years had conquered the local tribes and brought most of the southern half of England under their control. The springs at Bath were in the territory of the tribe, the Dobunni. It is believed they were one of the tribes that sought peace with the Romans and became allies.

The Romans Arrive

The Romans created a spa in Bath, building on top of the natural springs and adopting the local goddess Sulis, and the town grew up around it, the Romans called the town Aquae Sulis or 'waters of Sulis'. Although this name does not seem to have been used until the Antonine Itinerary.[5] Before that it may have just been called 'Aquae Calidae' or 'hot waters'.[6]

Bath does not seem to have ever been a big or major site for the Romans, it did not have a council or very large Roman administration. The main feature would have been the baths and the temple that were built later. Originally it was just the hot spring waters. Experts believe the building of the temple and sanctuary began around 70 AD onwards.

The sanctuary structure comprises of a fairly standard Roman bath system. A large hall to the south of the spring which could have been the frigidarium, flanked by two smaller rooms. A caldarium with two small, heated plunge baths and a tepidarium to the west of the hall. To the north and west of the caldarium there would have been furnace and service rooms. The entrance may have been to the southwest of the frigidarium which is where the apodyterium would have also been located.

On a visit to a Roman bath, you would begin in the changing room, the apodyterium. Your bathing began with a dip in the frigidarium, in the cold water, then the warmer waters of the tepidarium, and onto the caldarium which had the hottest waters. You would then visit each of the baths in reverse order finishing with the cold water and back to the apodyterium.

The baths at Bath followed the usual layout, but there is something extra to this particular site. There is a great hall and two further large rooms that contain three baths or decreasing size. These baths are filled with hot water coming direct from the springs. The large hall or the natation is the Great Bath that visitors are most familiar with today. It is surrounded by covered walkways with pillars and arcades. These areas had seating and would possibly have been used for relaxing, meeting and chatting with friends and playing games or eating snacks.

It is thought that architects were brought over from Gaul to design the temple, so we assume they also designed the buildings for the bathing sanctuary too.

There is a lot of historic and archaeological information about the building of the Roman Baths, but as we are focusing on Sulis specifically here I am only lightly touching on the edges of a huge subject. If you are interested in the history, it is a fascinating subject, and I would recommend looking at the Roman Baths website and there are several books on it listed at the end of this book.

The Temple

When you visit the Roman Baths as I have been lucky enough to do on numerous occasions, if you are seeking Sulis, the first thing that strikes you is the sculptured pediment of her temple. Built within the grounds of the Roman Baths north of the sacred spring, was a temple dedicated to Sulis. Not much of it remains now other than pieces of the pediment and some of the flooring and bits of altar. But you get a real sense of 'her' there. It is described as a 'great classical temple' with a portico of four high columns above its courtyard.[7] The columns sat on a podium approached by a flight of full width stone steps and supported a pediment filled with sculpture. Behind the portico would have been a main door.

Today you can sit at the top of a set of modern stairs and look directly at the pieced together pediment of the temple. They have placed the broken pieces together and filled in the rest with imagery. However, the main focus is the centre piece, what was originally known as 'the gorgon'. It was initially thought to be the image of a snake headed gorgon, but on much closer inspection the face is surrounded by hair and beard rather than snakes, although it could be wearing a snake headed torque around the neck. The Roman goddess Minerva apparently bore a slain Gorgon's head on her shield so that could be where the idea comes from. Myself, and others believe the face could be the solar god Belenus. I will leave it up to you to decide!

To the north of the sacred spring is a rectangular courtyard. At the west end you will find a temple dedicated to the goddess Sulis Minerva.

In the front of the temple was a lower paved area that extended around the spring and right up to the walls of the baths. Roman temples had a fanum, or sacred precinct that had specifically defined boundaries.

The pool in this area seems to have been open to the air but it may have been enclosed on the sides by tall upright slabs of stone. The suggestion is the spring was enclosed but also still visible suggesting that only those that had special permission or had carried out the correct rituals would be allowed inside the boundary.

The pediment was supported on four tall columns with a set of steps leading up to it. Inside the temple would have been a statue of the goddess Sulis Minerva. Also included would have been an altar in front of her statue, for her to 'look down upon'.

Rituals would have been carried out here, ceremonies and sacrifice around the altar facing the statue of the goddess. Gifts, offerings and petitions would be thrown into the hot spring pool that was also included within the temple boundaries.

Parts of the altar have been found and it appears to have been a tall, square stone platform with eight Roman deities carved into the four corners (two on each). Four of the gods are thought to be Bacchus, Hercules, Apollo and Jupiter. The other four have not been found. Were the other gods part of the roman Olympian gods set? A small part of stone that includes the shape of a trident was found near the remains of the altar, thought, perhaps, to be Neptune who is also one of the main team of deities, Minerva also being one of the top Roman gods.

Rituals would have been carried out around the altar along with sacrifices, perhaps with the idea that the statue of the goddess could overlook them along with the energy from her sacred spring.

At the end of the paved courtyard, you will find the temple which was 'domus deam' or 'house of the goddess' and was built and decorated to honour her in a worthy manner.

The belief is also that the temple was highly decorated with bright colours and gilded. The bronze head of a statue believed to be Sulis Minerva was uncovered in an archaeological dig. It is gilded and just slightly bigger than life size. The statue must have cast an imposing site, glittering in the flames from the fire.

Part of the baths consist of a large stone tank lined with lead sheets to waterproof it; archaeologists call this the 'sacred spring'. An inscription was found on lead that called the pool 'fons sulis' which translates to 'Spring of Sulis'.

The Gorgon's Head and the Pediment

Sitting proudly atop the pediment to Sulis's temple is a round plaque that features what appears to be a male face. Who or what it represents is an ongoing discussion. A few people feel that it represents a male deity, and that Sul is in fact a god, not a goddess. Although for me this theory does not work at all because the Romans equated Sulis with their goddess Minerva, they would not have done that if the resident hot springs deity was a male. Some suggest the image is of a god such as

Belenus, that greeted visitors as they came to pay their respects to the goddess Sulis. Others feel the image is that of a sun god. Another idea is that the image shows Bladud complete with wings and healing serpents. The premise of it being a sea god is also thrown into the mix, perhaps Neptune or Oceanus. There is the obvious watery connection. Alan Richardson puts forward the theory the image is the god Fontus.[8] The name derives from 'font' or 'source' and as a god of springs and wells it would fit quite nicely.

Paul Dunne suggests the image of the Gorgon's head to be that of Pontus, an ancient pre-Olympian sea god, one of the Greek primordial gods.[9] He also puts forward the idea that it would mean Sulis was the granddaughter of Gaia and daughter of Pontus. This puts a Greek spin on what I believe to be a wholly English deity, so personally this does not track for me, but it is obviously open to debate!

In 1890, the Rev Professor Sayce put forward the theory the image is of a sun god that presided over the entire Baths providing protection for all within.[10] The heat within the springs being provided by the sun and this sun god being the major deity for the entire venue. The goddess Sulis being the deity that ruled the healing spring enclosure within the main structure. I like this idea and it works for me; I give the sun god the name of Belenus.

The main blocks of the carved pediment were discovered in 1790 and they have been pieced together to form what would have been the pediment above the temple of Sulis. I find it intriguing that a lot of the pieces of stone are broken quite drastically, but the central round face is still intact in one whole piece. This depicts a male face and has been described as a typical Celtic male. Diodorus Siculus writing in the 1st Century states, *'their aspect is terrifying…they look like wood demons, their hair thick and shaggy like a horse's mane…some leave a moustache that covers the whole mouth'.*

The Bath head does resemble that description. But it also features large ears, two snakes, and angelic feathered wings. The eyes are prominent and clear, seemingly watching you intently. Originally this image was marked as a 'male Medusa' but now carries the label 'Gorgon's head' although it is obviously something quite different and very special. Heads were symbolic to the ancient Celts and images of them can be found in a lot of ancient sites. The ancient Celts were quite partial to head hunting, preserving the severed heads of their victims in cedar oil inside wooden boxes. Although Minerva also has strong connection to the Gorgon, she bore his slain head on her shield.

George Scharf, a Victorian scholar suggested the head image was the personification of the hot spring waters and he was not alone in this view.[11] This view was adapted and by the 20th century the idea became that the image was a conflation of Minerva's attribute of the Gorgon with a water god's face symbolising the sacred spring waters. Or is it just a protective image, like that of a severed head placed on the top of the pediment as a warning or a guardian of the waters?

Looking at the rest of the imagery on the pediment there are more nods to solar powers. There is a feel of power and victory with the artwork, it would have been very imposing to view originally. Is it perhaps the Romans making their stamp on the area, showing their might, conquest and strength? Maybe they were just showing off!

Disc – The face is set on a disc which could be a shield and is surrounded by a wreath of oak leaves. The oak was (and still is) a sacred tree, king of the trees in fact which could point to this character being full of victory and fertility. *Coronae civicae (civic crown)* were made of oak leaves and awarded to soldiers who rescued comrades in battle during the Republican period.[12]

After a coronae civicae was given to Augustus by the Senate in 27 BC they became an image of power. The oak is sacred to the god Belenus which brings in another connection to him. The shield shape could represent the military aspect and Rome's triumphs.

Eight-pointed star – Above the head is an eight-pointed star. A link to the heavens and the stars and planets? Stars were sometimes seen as symbols of divinity and the gods, however, in some cases they were used to note deified kings or emperors. Stars have been seen as emblems on statues of Julius Caesar and Octavian as well.

Victories – The disc is held by two winged Victories who are standing on globes. Victories appear frequently in military contexts in Britain, the image being introduced by Augustus after the Battle of Actium.[13] They symbolise imperial military victory. Victoria, derived from the Latin 'vincere' meaning 'to conquer' was a winged figure, a messenger from the gods bestowing praise to the victorious.[14] They were often depicted on images in pairs, they were used to represent the spirit of victory.

Tritons – Below the disc are two sea beings, often called Tritons. There is what seems to have been a torso draped with seaweed beneath the victory in the right-hand corner, thought to have been part of a Triton blowing on a conch shell. The second Triton would have been in the opposite corner. Triton can be found in Greek mythology, he is a demigod of the sea, son of Poseidon and Amphitrite.[15] He appears as a merman, half man and half fish. He can sometimes be found depicted as 'many' rather than just one and referred to as 'tritones', as we see in this imagery.[16]

Helmets – At the bottom are helmets, one in the shape of a dolphin's head, the other has an owl perched on top with two hands clasping his wings.

Owl – Often linked with the goddess Minerva and a symbol of wisdom.

Dolphin – Another animal often associated with Minerva.

Spheres – The Victories stand upon spheres; they do bear a resemblance to the world. The globes appear to be criss-crossed with lines, suggested to mark the paths of the planets.[17]

Overall, could this depict the sun as it passes through the seasons with the heavens and skies above and the sea and earth beneath and further below that the realms of the Underworld?

Belenus

Who is the god Belenus? He does seem to have been around in Britain before the Romans arrived. There is some archaeological evidence.

Mention of Belenus, or under the spelling Bellinus, is made on a buff sandstone building stone found at Piercebridge (Moribum) in Durham.[18] The inscription simply states 'Bellinus' and you do not need a translation for that!

A broken stone altar found at Overborough, Lancashire bears the text '[Nu]minib(us) [Au]g(usti) n(ostri) et Ge-[ni]o COLGF [A]poll[i]nis [B]ellinus v(otum) s(olvit) l(ibens) m(erito)' which translates as *'To the Divinities of our Emperor and the Genius of the guild of Apollo Bellinus willingly and deservedly fulfilled his vow.'*

Mention of Belenus is made in various ancient texts from across Europe. He is believed to have been widely worshipped throughout Britain and Europe. His name translates as *'bright or shining one'*. He looks to have been a solar deity, so he works nicely with Sulis. I have walked with Belenus for several years now and he is a powerful and strong deity.

The Façade of the Four Seasons

A number of pieces of stone have been found over the years that seem to be part of the same structure. Eventually it was pieced together to form what is believed to be a façade with fluted pilasters dividing the wall into spaces with a central space for a doorway. Each pilaster has a large niche roof with a shell canopy protecting a seated figure. Above each one is the image of a running cupid figure. The cupid figures each seem to be holding an item that has led experts to believe the façade represented the four seasons. Sadly, there are only small fragments of the seated figures, the only one that is identifiable seems to represent spring. There is an inscription running along the top of the façade, the part above spring can be seen and it reads *'C. Protacius...deae Sulis Minervae'*, 'Gaius Protacius of the goddess Sulis Minerva'. Cunliffe suggests this building was one of the temple structures.[19]

Altars and Dedications

Several altars and dedications have been found during the archaeological digs at the Roman baths covering various deities. These seem to have been dedicatory items. The majority of these are made from a stone called oolite. The word oolite comes from ancient Greek and means 'egg stone', it is a limestone consisting of a mass of grains (ooliths). It is a stone found in and around Bath and most of the buildings old and modern are built from it. It has a beautiful sandy light honey colour to it.

People would have flocked to the town, some from other parts of the Roman world. Some erected altars to their gods for their safe journey or their recovery or for some other service, while those less favoured by the gods died, only to be commemorated by their tombstones.[20]

I have listed here the ones that mention Sulis.

An oolite altar was found at Bath built into a wall in York Street opposite the Roman Baths.[21] The top and base were broken off and a moulding above the wording had been chiselled off. The inscription reads 'Q(uintus) Pompeius Anicetus Suli which' translates as *'Quintus Pompeius Anicetus to Sulis'.*

An imported white marble slab fragment was found near the Baths bearing the inscription 'Deae S[uli] Ti(berius) Cl(audius) T[i(beri) fil(ius)] Sollem[nis] [. .]' which translates as *'To the goddess Sulis Tiberius Claudius Sollemnis, son of Tiberius, …'*

An oolite altar with rectangular focus and plain sides was found near the spring of the hot bath bearing the inscription 'Deae Suli Mi-nervae Sulinus Matu-ri fil(ius) v(otum) s(olvit) l(ibens) m(erito)' which translates as *'To the goddess Sulis Minerva Sulinus, son of Maturus, willingly and deservedly fulfilled his vow.'*

An oolitic limestone statue base was found underneath the Pump Room at Bath. The statue base looks like an altar with a plain moulded capital and base, but the capital is flat topped and has no decoration which is usually found on an altar. It may have been a plinth for a statue. It bears the inscription 'deae Suli L(ucius) Marcius Memor harusp(ex) d(ono) d(edit)' which translates as *'To the goddess Sulis, Lucius Marcius Memor, soothsayer, gave (this) as a gift.'*

This one is particularly interesting as 'harusp(ex)' indicates a professional divination reader, one who inspects the entrails (human or animal?) to interpret the will of the Gods. It is believed to be the only find in Britain that indicates a professional diviner who read entrails.

An oolite dedication stone was found near the Great Bath, the top and base are broken away. It bears the inscription 'Priscus Touti f(ilius) lapidariu[s] cives Car[nu-] tenus Su[li] deae v(otum) [s(olvit) l(ibens) m(erito)]' which translates as *'Priscus, son of Toutius, stonemason, a tribesman of the Carnutes, to the goddess Sulis willingly and deservedly fulfilled his vow.'*

The Carnutes were a tribe who occupied a territory between the Seine and the Loire rivers in France.[22]

An oolite altar was found on the site of the Pump Room which reads 'Deae Suli [p]ro salute et [i]ncolumitate Aufidi Maximi (centurio) leg(ionis) VI Vic(tricis) M(arcus) Aufidius Lemnus libertus v(otum) s(olvit) l(ibens) m(erito)' and translates as *'To the goddess Sulis for the welfare and safety of Aufidius Maximus, centurion of the Sixth Legion Victrix, Marcus Aufidius Lemnus, his freedman, willingly and deservedly fulfilled his vow.'*

The Sixth Victorious Legion was founded by Octavian (the future emperor of Rome, Augustus) in 41 BC.[23] It is thought the Sixth Legion came over to Britain around 122 AD. The construction of the first bridge over the River Tyne at Newcastle is attributed to them. They also seem to have been involved in building many of the forts along Hadrian's Wall.

An oolite altar was found at Bath but the upper part is badly damaged. The inscription can be made out as 'Dea[e] Suli [o] b s[alutem] sạc(rum) G(ai) Iav[oleni Sa]tur[n-] [al]is [...] [i]m[a] g[in]n(iferi) leg(ionis) II Aug(ustae) Ḷ(ucius) Manius Dionisias libe(r)t(us) v(otum) s(olvit) l(ibens) m(erito)' and translates as *'To the goddess Sulis on behalf of the welfare of Gaius Javolenus Saturnalis, ... imaginifer of the Second Legion Augusta, Lucius*

Manius Dionisias, his freedman, willingly and deservedly fulfilled his vow.'

An 'imaginifer' was the bearer of a standard with the emperor's portrait. The Second Legion Augusta was part of the invasion force into Britain in 43 AD with Vespasianus in command.[24] The legion was split into smaller detachments and station in various forts throughout south-west Britain until 48 AD when a legionary fortress was built in Exeter. In 67 AD the legion was moved to Gloucester and in 75 AD onto South Wales. Most of the legion was involved in construction of Hadrian's Wall during 122 AD and 125 AD. They were also involved in building the Antonine Wall between 139 AD and 142 AD.

An oolite altar was found on the site of the Pump Room. Both pieces were in place, but it is broken diagonally. It bears the inscription '[D]eae Suli pro salute et incolumita-[te] Mar(ci) Aufid[i] [M]aximi (centurio) leg(ionis) VI Vic(tricis) [A]ufidius Eu-tuches leb(ertus) v(otum) s(olvit) l(ibens) m(erito)' and translates as *'To the goddess Sulis for the welfare and safety of Marcus Aufidius Maximus, centurion of the Sixth Legion Victrix, Aufidius Eutuches, his freedman, willingly and deservedly fulfilled his vow.'*

An oolite tombstone was found 800m northeast from the Roman Baths. It is shallow and the back is smooth. It bears the inscription 'D(is) M(anibus) G(aius) Calpurnius [R]eceptus sacer-dos deae Su-lis vix(it) an(nos) LXXV Calpurnia Trifo-sa l[i]bert(a) coniunx f(aciendum) c(uravit)' which translates as *'O the spirits of the departed; Gaius Calpurnius Receptus, priest of the goddess Sulis, lived 75 years; Calpurnia Trifosa, his freedwoman (and) wife, had this set up.'*

An oolite altar with plain sides was found in the cistern of the Cross Bath. It bears the inscription: 'Deae Su-li Min(ervae) et

Nu-min(ibus) Aug(ustorum) G(aius) Curiatius Saturninus (centurio) leg(ionis) II Aug(ustae) pro se su-isque v(otum) s(olvit) l(ibens) (erito)' Which translates as 'To the goddess Sulis Minerva and to the Divinities of the (two) Emperors Gaius Curiatius Saturninus, centurion of the Second Legion Augusta, willingly and deservedly fulfilled his vow for himself and his kindred.'

It is thought that the two emperors might be Marcus Aurelius and Verus.

Other Deities in the Roman Baths

Archaeological investigations have turned up evidence of dedications and requests made to several other deities within the baths. It suggests the site may have been more of a religious venue with people travelling and making offerings to their own personal deities as well as to Sulis. I have included some of them here:

Goddess Diana

An oolite base, perhaps from an altar with plain sides, found in the ruins of the Hot Bath. The inscription reads 'Dea(e) Dia|na(e) sacrati|ssima(e) votu|m solvit Vettius B[e]|5 nignus lib(ertus)' which translates as 'To the most hallowed goddess Diana Vettius Benignus, a freedman, fulfilled his vow.'

Genius Loci

An oolite altar quite damaged was found in the foundations of a market near the Guildhall in Bath, it reads 'Genio loci | [.] IΛ [ ] N P. | [..] | [..] | 5 [ ] leg(ionis) VI [Vic(tricis)] | Forianus | v(otum) s(olvit) l(aetus) l(ibens) m(erito)' which translates as 'To the Genius of this place ... of the Sixth Legion Victrix, Forianus gladly, willingly, and deservedly fulfilled his vow.'

Genius Loci means 'spirit of place' which was sometimes used when a person was unsure of which deity to all upon.[25] There are variations on genius being used to describe a personal guardian spirit or the spirit of a household, the idea was extended to cover the spirit guardians of a place, a building or an area.

Mars Loucetius and Nemetona

An oolite altar with plain sides was found in the lower part of Stall Street in Bath with the inscription 'Peregrinus | Secundi fil(ius) | civis Trever | Loucetio | 5 Marti et | Nemetona | v(otum) s(olvit) l(ibens) m(erito)' which translates as *'Peregrinus, son of Secundus, a Treveran, to Loucetius Mars and Nemetona willingly and deservedly fulfilled his vow.'*

Both these deities are Celtic and sometimes seen together in sites across Europe.

Luna

Part of the Façade of the Four Seasons seems to have included a pediment with the image of the goddess Luna featuring a crescent moon behind her head and a riding whip in one hand.[26] Her hair is piled on top of her head in a high bun and her dress is heavily draped. The corners of the pediment seem to have been carved with globes. This structure seems to have faced the temple of Sulis. Interesting to have a lunar goddess in a solar goddess temple, perhaps to bring about a balance of some sort?

The Ending of Aquae Sulis

As for the Roman Baths themselves, they were transformed over time but by the end of the fifth century there was little left of the city that the Roman's would recognise. Archaeologists have discovered that by 470 AD the baths were probably still standing but had not been used for decades. The surrounding monuments had been demolished and the surrounding houses were abandoned or in ruins. It seems offerings were still being made well into the 5th Century though, but the focus was on the spring enclosure with surrounding buildings being left to ruin.

Around 370-380 AD the main outdoor altar was buried under a new floor. The belief is that this was also the time when the bronze statue of Sulis Minerva was removed and had her head broken off. Did the head break in the destruction of the statue or was it purposely decapitated?

From around 410-420 AD the spring was still being used but the surrounding buildings were now not only ruins but had also been quarried for the stone to be used elsewhere. It is believed the final destruction was around 450 AD.

Gradually a lot of the remains were built over, in particular parts of the East Bath were covered over in the 10th and 11th centuries, mainly by the abbey that now stands there. The city grew over the remnants of the Roman baths, much of which is still covered by pavements, shops and houses.

In 1727 workmen were digging a trench for a sewer, this is when the bronze head of the Sulis Minerva statue was unearthed, although at the time they believed it to be of the god Apollo. This find began the interest in the site and intrigue as to what else lay there. The experts like to call this the beginning of the 'three-hundred-year dig'.[27] A lot of finds were made by workmen and builders, some noted down with detailed information and others not, with the building of newer structures continuing over the top. Various digs and excavations took place over time, some more successful than others. The most notable perhaps date from the 1970s/80s which have given us the structures and site that we see today. There have been a number of important people involved over the years, but I do want to give a shout out to Sir Barry Cunliffe who is one of the most respected and influential archaeologists involved in making the Roman Baths what they are now. I may also be a little bit 'fan girl' about him.

Offerings to the Spring

As humans we seem to have a need to throw things into water and the springs are no different. A huge number of items have been unearthed that were presumably given as offerings to the goddess into the hot waters of the spring.

Coins seem to have been the favourite with nearly 13,000 having been recovered ranging from small denominations up to very expensive gold coins. Was the offering of a few pieces of small change a reflection of the size of the request? If you were asking a great deal of the goddess, would you have given her a more expensive offering?

Personal items have also been found such as a gold earring, a cosmetic box, spindle whorls, bronze bracelets and bronze earrings, an ivory handled knife and several brooches. The jewellery items all seem to have belonged to females, but perhaps were given as appropriate gifts to a female deity.

Other items include an ingot of lead, parts of a crossbow and gemstones from ring settings. Items given as offerings perhaps from craftsmen or tradespeople. The gemstones are intriguing, there are thirty-three semi-precious stones and one glass, all believed to have been created by the same craftsman and found in a group near the east end of the Great Bath. The gems are all cut and engraved although they seem to be used and worn and would probably have been set into rings. The stones or 'intaglios' as they are known, are made from amethyst, carnelian and red jasper, each one intricately carved. Most of the images feature roman deities such as Apollo, Bonus Eventus, Mars, Ceres, Venus, Fortuna, Sol and Mercury. Did the person give their entire collection up to the goddess as an offering or did he lose them accidentally?

A tin mask was also recovered and a small ivory upper torso carving. The torso could have been given as an ex-voto or representation of illness and requesting healing. The mask may have been given to ask for healing for a facial issue, but it could also be a ceremonial item that was offered to the goddess.

Pewter vessels have also been found, bowls and small handled dishes some of which are inscribed with the words

'Deae Suli Minerva' which translates as 'to the goddess Sulis Minerva'. Twenty-one pewter, two silver and one bronze vessel have been unearthed so far. The paterae, or small handed dishes as most of them are, could have been offerings to the goddess or given to the spring waters in a ritual disposal if they were old or broken. One of the pewter items is an inkwell and another is a candlestick decorated with the shape of a deer.

Some of the cups have names around the rim, these form a pattern that represents Hadrian's Wall and the Roman forts that were spaced along its length. Some of the cups also have remnants of coloured enamel decoration. Could these have been early souvenirs from the wall? Does the presence of cups also mean that liquid offerings were given to the goddess, wine perhaps?

Two pieces found, a silver gilt sceptre finial and a plaque of filigree could have been from ceremonial items. Ritual items cast into the waters at the end of their lives or maybe accidental.

An interesting find is that of a penannular brooch, dated around the 5th Century. Experts believe it to be from Ireland. The crafting features birds and fish, are these just from an old Irish myth or were they part of Sulis' legend?

The Curses

It is the curses that seem to be mentioned the most when referring to the offerings for Sulis. To date, 130 curse tablets have been recovered. Written with a metal nib or point, generally on a small piece of pewter or lead then rolled or folded and consigned to the waters. Most of them are asking for vengeance on someone that had wronged them, and they even give lists of possible suspects. A lot of them seem to be about personal items such as the theft of a towel. The curse tablets found in the spring at Bath, also known as 'defixiones', range in date from the 2nd to the late 4th century AD.[28]

Dan Jordan sets a scene for us:[29]

When Gaius stepped naked from the bath at Aquae Sulis, he found out his cloths had been stolen. He was left naked, wet, and desperate. The thief had disappeared and_ according to the writers of the Roman_ no policeman would ever find the thief.[30] At the very best, they could determine a penalty, as harsh as labor in the mines of the bathhouse, in case the thief were a civilian. For a Roman soldier, the penalty would be immediate, dishonorable discharge from service. For Greeks, too, burglary counted as a civil offense. However, stealing someone's clothes from the bath would be punished by death IF you got caught. As Gaius waited for his friend or slave to bring him a new suit of clothes, suffering the injustice, he decided to enact a legal fiction and donate his stolen clothes to the goddess of the waters Sulis Minerva. Gaius urged Sulis to find the thief and to torture him until he would return her own clothes to her.

Sending or requesting curses from the divine was a common practice for our ancestors and can be found in many cultures. It shows the belief or perhaps the superstition that the divine could not only answer your prayers for positive requests but also listen and bring down fury upon those that had wronged you.

The terminology of the practice of magic in antiquity is subtle, varied, and specific at the same time. The most frequent term in this terminology is defixio_ with the plural form of defixiones or defixionis_ which means "enchantment" or "a binding", from the Latin verb defigo, meaning "to fasten".[31]

The language used on the curse tablets varies with Roman capital letters, old Roman cursive, new Roman cursive and one tablet that has both old and new Roman cursive letters.[32] One of the tablets has been written in a language that no one can identify, some suggest it is in ancient Brythonic, others that it is just marks given to look like writing.[33]

There are experts who suggest the text on curse tablets included magical words and symbols, some even being written back to front.[34] The idea has also been put forward that curse tablets may have been nailed to the temple wall where they could be seen by everyone. Others being folded or rolled and sent into the waters so that only the goddess could read it. More than half of the names on the curse tablets are Celtic, the rest are Roman.

What needs to be remembered with these tablets is that most of them are very badly written with spelling and grammar mistakes throughout. This does not help when it comes to translating them and making sense of the writing. Experts suggest most of them were written by those lower in society that would not have had much schooling. Even those that were well educated may not have been given proper instruction in spelling or grammar. That would make sense in the case of the unreadable curse tablet that just has marks on in an unrecognisable language, was this person illiterate but still wanted to write a request to the goddess?

A lot of the tablets have been damaged, have parts missing or are now in part unreadable, but here are some examples:

A lead sheet found in the reservoir under the King's bath, found in 1880.[35]

Which translates to *'May he who carried off Vilbia from me become as liquid as water. (May) she who obscenely devoured her (become) dumb, whether Velvinna, Exsupereus, Verianus, Severinus, A(u)gustalis, Comitianus, Catus, Minianus, Germanilla (or) Jovina.'* The suggestion is that Vilbia is a Celtic woman's name. Was the woman a slave, a wife or a concubine, we do not know. The other suggestion is that Vilbiam, as it is written is not a name but an object, a pointed tool. Perhaps we will never know.

Another lead alloy tablet, written in Latin capitals, translated reads:[36]

'I have given to the goddess Sulis the six silver coins which I have lost.

It is for the goddess to exact (them) from the names written below Senicianus and Saturniuns and Anniola.'

A lead alloy tablet written on both sides and folded twice, translates to read:

On one side – *'The person who lifted my bronze vessel is utterly accursed. I give (him) to the temple of Sulis, whether woman or man, whether slave or free, whether boy or girl, and let him who has done this spill his own blood into the vessel itself.'*

On the other side – *'I give, whether woman or man, whether slave or free, whether boy or girl, that thief who has stolen the property itself (that) the god may find (him).'*

A lead alloy tablet written on both sides but not folded. This tablet has the text written in reverse order, the first letter inscribed in the first line is the last letter of the text and vice versa. It also has the addition of quoting 'whether Pagan or Christian' when identifying the thief.

On one side – *'Whether pagan or Christian, whether man or woman, whether boy or girl, whether slave or free, whoever has stolen from me, Annianus (son of) Matutina (?), six silver coins from my purse, you, Lady Goddess, are to exact (them) from him. If through some deceit he has given me…and do not give thus to him but reckon as (?) the blood of him who has invoked this upon me.'*

On the other side – *'Postumianus, Pisso, Locinna, Alauna, Materna, Gunsula, Candidina, Euticius, Peregrinus, Latinus, Senicianus, Avitianus, Victor, Scotius, Aessicunia, Paltucca, Callipsis, Celerianus.'*

He names all the suggested suspects, there are eighteen of them, was he just overly suspicious or hedging his bets?

A rectangular tablet cut from an alloy sheet, inscribed on both sides, then folded in half, unfortunately the writing on the outside has all but worn away.[37] *'To the goddess Sulis...whether slave or free, (if) whoever he shall be, you are not to permit him eyes or health unless blindness and childlessness so long as he shall live, unless (he...) these to the temple.'* I do not know what the accused did but the person writing the curse was definitely angry.

Two cojoining fragments scribed on an alloy sheet with a raised edge, reads *'(the person) who (has stolen) (my) horse blanket (?), whether (man or) woman, whether slave (or free) ... goddess Sulis.'*

An irregular shaped piece of cast alloy sheet hammered flat before inscribing on both sides with a blunt stylus. This was not folded but appears to have been pierced with a nail. Translated, it reads *'...I, Arminia, complain to you, Sulis, (that) you consume Verecundinius (son of) Terentius, who has (stolen...) two silver coins from me. You are not to permit (him) to sit or lie (or...or) to walk (or) (to have) sleep (or) health, (since) you are to consume (him) as soon as possible; and again...(not) to reach...'*

Two cojoining fragments of an irregular rectangle of cast alloy sheet, broken at what appears to be a fold, translated to read *'Oconea to the goddess Sulis M(inerva). I give you a pan (?). If anyone (has stolen) it...'* Oconea probably being the person's name, possibly Gaulish.

Two cojoining fragments of a rectangle alloy sheet, written with a stylus in mirror image letters, it keeps to the line sequence but reverses the order of letters in each line. It translates to read *'Lovernisca (gives) him who, whether (man) or woman, whether boy or girl (who) has stolen (her) cape.'* Lovernisca seems to have been a Celtic woman's name.

An irregular oval shape piece of molten lead inscribed with a blunt stylus, translates to read *'To the goddess Sulis. If anyone has stolen the bathing tunic of Cantissena, whether slave or free...'* Cantissena is probably a male name, possibly Celtic.

A cast alloy rectangle sheet which has been hammered, translates to read *'To Minerva the goddess Sulis I have given the thief who has stolen my hooded cloak, whether slave or free, whether man or woman. He is not to buy back this gift unless with his own blood.'*

Five pieces of an irregular rectangle cut from tin alloy sheet and inscribed with a blunt stylus, although badly corroded, translates to read *'Exsuperius gives an iron pan (?). (The person) who...innocence for him...of (?) Sulis, whether man (or woman), whether slave or free...this...and...have stolen his...whether, man or woman, is to have given satisfaction with their blood. You are to reclaim (?) this (if) anyone has stolen the vessel from me.'*

A rectangle cut from thick alloy sheet and inscribed, translates to read *'Uricalus, Docilosa his wife, Docilis his son and Docilina, Decentinus his brother, Alogiosa: the names of those who have sworn (who have sworn) at the spring of the goddess Sulis on the 12th of April. Whosoever has perjured himself there you are to make him pay for it to the goddess Sulis in his own blood.'* This one is slightly different in that it is not a curse but a sanction against perjury with a sworn oath. Uricalus seems to be a Celtic name, Docilis/ Docilosa/Docilina/Decentinus are all Latin. Alogiosa unusual and possibly from ancient Greek.

These are just some examples of the 130 curse tablets found. As you can see there is a familiar theme running through a lot of them.

Haruspex

One of the inscriptions found in Bath reads *'To the Goddess Sulis, Lucius Marcuis Memor, haruspex, gave this gift.'* A haruspex was a soothsayer, a seer that could foretell the future, specifically using the entrails of animals but often by reading the fire or smoke. The haruspex originated with the Etruscans but was brought into Roman practice.[38] They were common in ancient Rome right up until the reign of Emperor Constantine, as a Christian he brought in a ban on all forms of divination.

Was the haruspex a permanent fixture in the Roman Baths or was he just a visitor? Sadly, we do not have an answer to that question. There was a practice where the haruspex visited other places in order to give advice and readings.

The word haruspex brings together the Latin word 'haru' and the Greek word for 'gut' added to the Latin word 'spex' which means 'to look'.[39] Basically, haruspex translates as *'one who looks at guts'*. This type of divination is referred to as augury, along with less gruesome variations such as reading the flight of birds or the movement of the stars.

We do know there was priests of Sulis in residence, from a memorial altar found nearby that gives us the name of Gaius Calpunius Receptus, Priest of the Goddess Sulis.

An oolite tombstone, altar shaped found in Bathwick near the Roman Baths with the inscription 'D(is) M(anibus) | G(aius) Calpurnius | [R]eceptus sacer|dos deae Su|5 lis vix(it) an(nos) LXXV | Calpurnia Trifo|sa l[i]bert(a) coniunx | f(aciendum) c(uravit)' which translates as *'To the spirits of the departed; Gaius Calpurnius Receptus, priest of the goddess Sulis, lived 75 years; Calpurnia Trifosa, his freedwoman (and) wife, had this set up.'*

The Eternal Flame

This quote from the 3rd century Roman geographer, Solinus is interesting:

Minerva is the patroness of these springs. In her shrine, the perpetual fires never whiten into ashes. When they dwindle away, they change into stony globules.

Could it suggest that an eternal flame was kept alight in the temple of Sulis? Was it in the form of a fire as the wording implies? It would be another nod to the fire and solar connection for the goddess Sulis.

King Bladud

One of the myths that surrounds the city of Bath and the creation of the Baths, and the Temple lies in a story written by Geoffrey of Monmouth.[40] The story is obviously not based on fact because the Romans really did build the Baths, but it is an interesting tale, nonetheless.

There is a small statue of King Bladud within the King's Bath dating back to the 18th Century, entitled 'Bladud, son of Lud Hudibras, 8th king of the Britons, first discoverer and founder of these Baths'. The description is lifted straight from Monmouth's work *History of the Kings of Britain*.

Monmouth writes:

Next succeeded Bladud, his son, and reigned twenty years. He built Kaerbadus, now Bath, and made hot baths in it for the benefit of the public, which he dedicated to the goddess Minerva; in whose temple he kept fires that never went out nor consumed to ashes, but as soon as they began to decay were turned into balls of stone. About this time the prophet Elias prayed that it might not rain upon earth; and it did not rain for three years and six months. This prince was a very ingenious man, and taught necromancy in his kingdom, nor did he leave off pursuing his magical operations, till he attempted to fly to the upper region of the air with wings which he had prepared, and fell upon the temple of Apollo, in the city of Trinovantum, where he was dashed to pieces.[41]

Monmouth may have drawn inspiration from the writings of Tysilio whose description seems incredibly similar.[42]

And after him came Blaiddyd, his son; and he reigned twenty years. And he built Kaer Vaddon, and the baths which were always warm for the healing of any that had need of them. And he sacrificed to the sorceress called Minerva; he kindled fire that never died until it had burned down to fine ashes, and when it began to burn out, it rekindled the [second*] time in balls of fire. And at this time the prophets prayed that god would give no rain, and there was not a drop of rain for three years and seven months. And Blaiddyd was a deeply learned man. And he was the first in all Ynys Brydain who brought in necromancy; nor did he rest from practicing such arts until he made pinions and wings for himself and flew to the upper air, from thence he fell down on the temple of Apolo in Llyndain and was dashed in a hundred pieces.

Kaer Vaddon being the name for the city of Bath, Ynys Brydain being Britain and Llyndain the city of London.

There are variations to the story throughout history but most of them seem to include several points. Those being that Bladud could fly by magical means, he practised necromancy and fire and solar magic and worked with astrology. Is his name a nod to the god Belenus? Does he represent the Druids as a Pagan leader? I do not have answers, just thought-provoking questions!

And then the pigs appear in the story. Just to confuse the issue there are variations on where this part of the story came from too. In 1673 the mayor of Bath, Henry Chapman printed a rhyming appendix in his book, *Thermae redivivae*. His story, told of prince Bladud being outcast from his father's palace, contracts leprosy. He is forced to work as a lowly swineherd and in doing so his disease spreads to the pigs. The pigs, however, who are incredibly intelligent creatures find their way to the natural hot springs and bath in the waters and are cured. Bladud realising what has happened, follows suit and baths in the hot springs himself and is also miraculously cured. He returns home and builds the city of Bath at the site of the springs in celebration.

Then Bladud did the Pigs invect [infect], who grunting ran awayAnd vound whot [found hot] waters prezently, which made um vresh [them fresh] and gay.

Bladud was not so grote a Vool [great a fool], but zeeing [seeing] what Pig nid[need?] doe,

He beath'd [bathed] and wash'd and rins'd and beath'd from Noddle [head] down totoe.

Bladud was now (Gramercy [thanks] Pig) a delicate Vine [fine] boy, So whome [home] he trudges to his Dad, to be his only Joy.

And then he bilt this gawdy Town[43]

Is this just a bit of clever marketing by the mayor to raise the profile of the hot springs in the town?

There is a slightly earlier version of the story that gives the origins as 'traditional'. Although published originally anonymously, the suggestion is it was written by Robert Gay in 1666.

Bladud [...] became a swineherd near Bathe, which was then a bogg [...] of hotwater, in which his swine often wallowed, and one of them [...] was thereby cured, whereupon Bladon [sic] [...] was also cured, whereupon he built a Temple, and consecrated it to the sun, as God of the heat of the Bath-water.[44]

It is worth noting here that pigs and wild boar were very important animals to the ancient Celtic peoples. It was believed they had a strong connection and gateway to the Underworld.

The name Bladud has been spelt in various ways over the years whether in translations, mis spelling or changes in language, but you will find it as: Bladud, Bladuth, Blaidydd, Baldud, Beldud, Bladus or Bledud. The important part is the root of the name, Bla, Bal or Bel. This is often associated with fire or bright, Bel being a word relating to the god of fire or light. There is a definite solar or fiery connection with the name.

For the last part of the name, this could be translated in various ways such as the Irish and Gaelic 'a god' or the Welsh 'mediator or arbitrator'. It may even have its roots in the Gaulish or Welsh meaning of 'druid'.

The Blending

The Romans often blended the native deities with their own. Perhaps it was to help the locals accept the Romans and welcome them in or maybe the Romans believed it was worthwhile making friends with the local gods. It does seem to have been a two-way process, we accepted some of their traditions and they adopted some of ours. There seems to have been a religious tolerance from the Romans to any groups that they did not feel threatened by. The Druids for instance were not tolerated, perhaps because they felt they were too organised and troublesome and sadly they paid for it with the Romans destroying them and their places of worship.

The Romans had their own pantheon of deities although most of these were adapted from the Greek gods, whose influence can be seen throughout their culture. The Romans also melded aspects of many other cultures particularly those of Eastern origin into their own. The base of their beliefs, however, was in the power of the Otherworld.

Minerva and Her Severed Head

The Romans saw that Sulis had similar attributes and characteristics to that of one of their own goddesses, Minerva. Thus, Sulis became double barrelled in the form of Sulis Minerva. I think it is important to note that Sulis comes first in the name. They obviously realised just how important she was to the local people.

In fact, in a lot of ancient scripts and writings, we find that Roman writers often referred to deities from other cultures using the names of the Roman gods, those that were more familiar to the writer.[45] He would use the name of a Roman god that had similar attributes to the unfamiliar deity.

The pagan deities found in ancient Briton did perhaps confuse the Romans a little. We did not have a structure to our 'pantheon'. There was no obvious hierarchy, they did not have mother and father gods and those that related directly to each season. Although Britain should probably have had a rain god!

Our deities were often localised and specific to one river or mountain and their characteristics changed with the passing of the seasons.

Minerva

I am only going to briefly touch on the goddess Minerva here, to give you an idea of her characteristics and attributes so that you can relate them to Sulis.

Minerva is a Roman goddess of crafts and trades.[46] She is one of the three deities of the Capitoline Triad who shared a temple on Capitoline Hill at Rome. Originally Jupiter, Mars and Quirinus the triad was later changed to Jupiter, Juno Regina and Minerva. As Minerva Medica she was goddess of doctors. Originally believed to be of Etruscan origin and then called Menrva or Menerva, she is goddess of wisdom, weaving, science, the arts and written laws.[47]

The Greek influence equated her to their goddess of war, Athene so Minerva became a goddess of war and strategy too.

The Waters

The bathing aside and even perhaps the deities too, the most important feature of the baths is the water. A magical endless flow of hot water from beneath the earth is definitely something to get excited about. Springs, wells and water in general have been revered by humans throughout the centuries. Water is a source of life and seen as places of wonder that held the energy, power and blessings of the gods. Looking into the history of deities in England in particular, the gods have all seemingly evolved from specific parts of the natural landscape. Water in particular conjures up spirits, nymphs and ultimately gods, whether it is a well, a spring or a river. Water has the ability to provide food and nourishment for us as humans, but also to water the land to grow crops. Water in the form of larger rivers also has the power to take life too. Water is life, but also death so it forms a cycle of life, death and rebirth. Water brings fertility and a connection to the bounty that Mother Earth provides. Wells and springs have also long been seen as portals to the Otherworld and realms. They are mystical liminal places that provide an opening to another place. Our ancestors understood nature, the changes in the seasons and even it seems a good grasp on moon and sun phases. They had a connection to the land, they needed to in order to survive.

Even looking at how the Romans set up the baths could be seen in a magical or even religious way. Bathing is as we know a socially acceptable need so that we stay clean and do not smell. But bathing also links to cleansing and purification, not just physically but mentally and spiritually too. The waters at Bath were also believed to be healing, this gives it a magical spin too. The offerings given up to the springs in Bath are an obvious sign that the waters were deemed to be magical.

Her Name

There is a debate about what the name Sulis translates to. The proto-Celtic translates of the word 'Suli' does seem to mean 'Sun'.[48] In Gaelic 'suil' means 'an eye', an opening or an orifice.[49] Other suggestions lean towards the name meaning 'eye', 'eye gap', 'vision' or 'well'. In Gaelic the word 'suileath' translates as *'sharp sighted and knowing'*. These could relate to the solar energy at the springs and perhaps even the idea that Sulis was 'all seeing'. In Welsh and old Irish the word 'suil' or 'sulis' means eye, gap or orifice.[50]

The author Phil Quinn suggests that wells in Celtic mythology were seen as the eye of an earth deity.[51] In fact, the Welsh word for eye, 'Llyad' is also used when describing the source of a river or stream.

The Latin name given to the site Aquae Sulis breaks down to mean 'The waters of Sulis'. The suggestion is that it translates completely to mean 'The waters of the gap' or 'the waters of the goddess of the gap'.[52]

Naming a goddess after an area or a description are very common. Dr Anne Ross writes:

> *springs, wells and rivers are of first and enduring importance as a focal point of Celtic cult practice and ritual...the Celtic mother goddesses, who frequently function in the role of war goddesses and prognosticators, have widespread association with water.*[53]

Sulis, the solar goddess, protector of the healing waters and judge and jury for those who were wronged. The solar energy obviously brings the characteristics that we associate with the element of fire, the all-seeing perhaps leads her to help with divination and seership. I think her rule over curses and the heat of the water from underground also gives her a link perhaps even to the Underworld.

Worship

I hesitate to use the word worship because that is not how I see my connection to deity. I do not bow down and worship the ground or any deity in particular. I prefer to see it as me walking beside the deity and honouring them and their power. But worship is a more recognisable description and probably more akin with how our ancestors revered and honoured the gods.

There was a certain amount of bargaining and even perhaps haggling with the gods particularly when it came to asking them for their energy. There are a number of altars dedicated to Sulis in the Roman Baths that have been set up as a thank you to the goddess for granting their request. In the format of 'I ask you for something, you grant it, so I pay for an altar in your honour'. It is an exchange of energy, much like the process we work with as modern-day Pagans. There must always be a system of checks and balances when working with spells and magic. You ask for something therefore you must give in return, to keep asking for the good stuff to manifest and not being thankful or grateful in return can totally upset the energy of things. Not that I am suggesting we build stone altars each time a spell has a positive result, of course.

The number of offerings that have been unearthed not just in the waters of Bath but in most springs and wells shows that people gave something in the hope of their wish or request being granted.

Offerings are in a way a sacrifice. The Roman Empire did put a ban on human sacrifice, although I am sure it still happened on occasion. Although animals were often sacrificed to the gods in the form of offerings but also to be able to read their entrails for divination purpose. Any type of offering is a sacrifice though, particularly if it is an item that is worth something to you. It could be in the form of food from your table or items of monetary value. There are all forms of exchange in energy.

Suleviae

I am including some information here about what seems to be a group of goddesses called the Suleviae. There is some archaeological evidence for them, one item being found at the site of the Roman baths. I include them as I have seen mention they might be a version of the goddess Sulis. I have found no evidence of this, and most experts seem to think they were a group of mother goddesses with no connection to Sulis.

An oolite statue base was found Bath (Aquae Sulis) with the inscription 'Sulevis Sulinus Sculptor Bruceti f(ilius) sacrum f(ecit) l(ibens) m(erito)' which translates as *'To the Suleviae Sulinus, a sculptor, son of Brucetus, gladly and deservedly made this offering.'*

A green sandstone base was found at Colchester (Camulodunum) with the inscription 'Matribus Sulevis Similis Atti f(ilius) ci(vis) Cant(iacus) v(otum) l(ibens) s(olvit)' which translates as '*To the Mother Goddesses Suleviae, Similis, son of Attus, a tribesman of the Cantiaci, willingly fulfilled his vow.*' Inscriptions can be found across Great Britain and parts of Europe.

The name translates as '*good guides*' or '*good rulers*'. The general consensus seems to be they are mother goddesses, some suggest sisters. They are guardians of the house and home.

PART II

Working with Sulis

What Do We Know?

We need to piece together bits and pieces to get an overall picture of Sulis and even this is a bit sketchy, but this is what I believe:

- She is local to Bath, dedications, offerings and mentions of her name are only found in Bath.
- She is a goddess of the hot springs.
- She accepted and presumably actioned curses.
- She is called upon to make judgement and justice.
- She is possibly a healing deity.
- As her name translates to gap or eye this leads me to connect her with seer abilities.
- The evidence of a haruspex on site may point to her being called upon for divination skills.
- Her connection to water brings in fertility.
- I also see her as a solar deity.
- Some evidence suggests she was called upon to aid in war and military strategy.
- There is some evidence to suggest there was an eternal flame burning in her temple.

Call Upon Her For

Blessings, courage, cleansing, creativity, cursing, divination, prophecy, finding lost things, healing, judgement, justice, knowledge, oaths, planning, psychic abilities, strategy, strength, warrior energy, wisdom.

Correspondences

Pigs
Dolphins
Owl

Sun
Solar cross
Gorgon head image
Water
Fire
Coins

For me, the solar cross and any kind of sun imagery suits her well. I know she is obviously associated with water, but the sun seems to be the dominant feature for me. I may have also spent an obscene amount of money in the Roman Baths shop, and now own a plaque with the 'gorgon' image on, a ceramic gorgon head chalice and several reproduction Roman coins that bear the image of Sulis (amongst other things I have purchased on each occasion). All of these things I use on my altar. I have also bought reproduction Roman coins at the Fishbourne Roman Palace in Chichester, Sussex, that I use as offerings.

The colours I use are again all solar connected, primarily yellow and red but I often bring in the bluey green colour of water as an accent.

I find her a strong and kick butt kinda goddess. She does not stand any nonsense of any kind. She is fiery but can always be appeased with a gift. I have never done it with any goddess before, but I feel the need to address her as M'lady. Each time I meditate to see her, she is always in the setting of the Roman Baths, I have never seen her in any other place. Although I do feel her walking with me all the time. She is ancient, very ancient, but I do believe she loved the arrival of the Romans, they gave her the attention she required and the beautiful temple she deserved.

When you connect with her and build a relationship, she will kick things into action very quickly. In my experience she gets things moving at a rapid pace. Do not call on her unprepared, be ready for a fast and furious journey!

With such a lack of information about her, you will need to make your own connections and build a relationship with her, as you should with any deity really. I find the best place to start with any new deity is to research. Thankfully the Roman Baths do have at least some archaeological finds that refer to her, so it gives you a starting point. After that you will need to make contact. Setting up an altar is a good way to begin, and meditation is always an excellent way in.

Sulis sits smack bang in the centre of a natural heated spring, which would usually lead you to the idea she is a healing goddess. I am not sure this was her main function; in fact, it does not sit right for me. I am sure the waters were thought to be healing, but I do not believe it was one of the main attributes of Sulis. Often at ancient sites where there is a well, a spring or sacred water you will find items given up to the waters that represent the body part that needs healing. For instance, if you had a dodgy leg, you might carve the shape of a leg (albeit in miniature) and give that as an offering. If you suffered from headaches, you might offer just the head of a small ornament to the waters. They were representations of the site on the body that the person was asking the deity to heal. Bath does not have these offerings, at least not that have been found yet, at some point in the future I may stand corrected. Only one small torso figure has been unearthed (so far).

Sir Barry Cunliffe writes:

> *At some healing springs it was quite usual for the sick and lame to dedicate to the deity a model, usually in wood, of whatever part of their anatomy was diseased. Deposits of arms, legs, eyes and other parts have been found...Bath is devoid of offerings of this type except for the single piece of ivory carved stylistically in the form of breasts. If, however, wooden ex votos had been thrown in they would have floated away when the sluice was open.*[54]

Does this mean that every single ex voto offered to the springs floated away?[55] Or that Sulis was not seen as a healing deity? I do not have an answer to that, but there have been no wooden offerings found at the Bath springs (so far). However, with the power of the element of water and the fact they are naturally warm, it does lead to a healing energy. With the water connection I think you can list healing as one of her correspondences, but I do not believe it was her main role or even one of her main attributes, you may feel differently!

I do feel strongly that she is all about justice. With the amount of curse tablets found she was obviously sought to make judgement on people and their actions. This could, of course, be seen as vengeance but again I do not feel that either, the requests were made for her to make the call of justice rather than smiting people you did not like.

With the waters coming from an 'eye' in the ground and the name Sulis being so strongly connected with the translation of eye, all seeing and knowing she has a strong seer quality. Add to that the haruspex who was obviously on site at the Baths Sulis seems to lend her energies to divination. She is one that I request assistance from for readings and divination of all kinds. There is a knowledge and wisdom quality to her personality for sure.

Sir Barry Cunliffe also suggests there is a war like side to Sulis, echoed in the characteristics of Minerva who had a martial side to her. But there are also some hints to her warrior energies. Cunliffe writes:

The washer from a model ballista could well have been an offering made by a soldier as thanks for some service the goddess had rendered, or in anticipation of help. That Bath was evidently popular among the army is shown by the number of military tombstones in the vicinity put up long after the garrison moved on. Perhaps they were of soldiers who had returned to the city in their retirement to settle, or of the wounded making a pilgrimage in anticipation of a cure.[56]

If we look at the attributes to the goddess Minerva, that we have more information for it also adds a few skills to Sulis' curriculum. If the Romans felt they were similar then we can draw from that. Minerva brought wisdom and knowledge, the arts and creativity – all of which tie in nicely with the idea that Sulis is a solar deity. This also brings in the energy and characteristics of the element of fire.

The suggestion that Sulis had an eternal flame or fire in her temple is interesting and makes perfect sense, she obviously had a strong connection to fire. But what is an eternal flame? The idea is a flame, or a fire is kept in a temple dedicated to deity, one that is constantly tended and never allowed to go out. An example can be found in Kildare in Ireland where a perpetual fire dedicated to Brigit was kept alight by nuns and holy women.[57] In Rome we find the Vestal Virgins who had the duty of watching and tending the sacred hearth of the flame in the temple of Vesta.[58]

This connects very nicely to working with candle magic. Having a candle dedicated to Sulis works well too, you can create your own and use it on a regular basis when you wish to connect with her. Whilst you do not need to keep the flame alight eternally, because that would not be safe, you can use it regularly to connect with Sulis.

Creating a Sulis Candle

If you are super talented you might like to create a candle from scratch. If like me, you have tried it, made a huge mess and ruined a number of decent saucepans then you may prefer to decorate a ready-made candle. Either way you will be adding your own energy and that of Sulis to a candle for you to use.

Choose a candle shape and size, I suggest a pillar, long taper or jar candle. You want it to be a decent size, big enough to decorate easily and to last a long while. You will be lighting this regularly so it needs to be of a size that will burn for a good few hours overall.

Start by cleansing the candles just to clear away any negative energy that it might have picked up on its journey to you. For Sulis it seems right to cleanse the candle using water, pass the candle briefly under running water or sprinkle with water. If you have some solar water that you charged under the sun it would be perfect, but you can use bottled spring or tap water. Visualise any negative energy being released as you do so.

Once your candle is cleansed you might like to charge it with solar energy. Leave the candle out under the waxing or full sun, just for a short while, you do not want the candle to melt in the hot sun.

Then you need to indicate the candle belongs to Sulis. I like to do this in various ways, each of which also becomes part of the dressing and decoration for the candle. You can use all of some of these ideas or add your own.

Carving – using a sharp knife, or I use a tattoo needle from one of my ritual tattoos and carve a symbol into the side of the candle. I often use a solar cross which is an equal arm cross surrounded by a circle. Or you could carve the symbol or representation for the sun. If you prefer you could carve the initial 'S' for Sulis or her full name down the side of the candle.

Anointing – choose an essential oil or oil blend you associate with Sulis and dress the candle with it. If you are going to roll the candle in crushed herbs, you do need to dress it with oil first to help the herbs to stick. Dip your finger or a small brush into your chosen oil and rub the oil from the bottom of the candle to the centre and from the top of the candle down to the centre. If your candle is in a container and the candle slips out, you can still dress it with oil. If it is set into a jar, you can add a few drops of oil to the top of the candle.

Herbs and Spices – Once anointed with oil you can roll your candle in a mixture of crushed herbs and spices. If your candle is in a jar, you can sprinkle some of the herb mixture on top instead. For large pillar candles you can sprinkle the herb mixture on top of the candle and then seal them in place by dripping wax from a lighted taper candle over the top.

Note: Be mindful that adding oils and herbs to your candle can cause the flame to spit and flare. Large pieces of herb can also catch light. Never leave a lit candle unattended.

Art – If you prefer you could paint or draw images onto the outside of your candle, these could be symbols, words or sigils.

Crystals – Small crystal chips can be added to the top of your candle by pushing them into the wax or placing them on top and dripping wax over them. Please bear in mind these crystal chips can get hot and may crack.

Leaves and Flowers – small, pressed flowers and leaves can be added to the side of your candle. Melt a little candle wax and dip a little brush into it, brush a small amount of the melted wax onto the back of your flower or leaf and press it onto the candle. You can brush further melted wax over the top to seal them.

Dedicating – once you have finished your creation you can dedicated the candle to Sulis. I like to do this with a little blessing. Light your candle and say your blessing, allow the candle to burn for a while. Let it burn until the wax has melted to the full width of the candle, this will allow it to burn fully and properly when you use it again.

Now say a blessing, state out loud that this candle has been created for and is dedicated to the goddess Sulis. You can just speak words from your heart or create a chant, such as:

This candle I have now created
I dedicate it to the goddess Sulis
With each light of the candle flame
I invoke Sulis and ask for her by name

Then snuff out the flame. The candle is now dedicated to the goddess Sulis and can be kept on your altar. Light it each time you wish to connect with her, seek her advice, call upon her energy or meditate to meet with her.

Once your candle is used, make sure you keep enough of a stub to be able to light a new candle wick from your old one. This way you are passing the eternal flame and transferring the energy of the old candle onto the new one.

Each time you light it to connect with the goddess you may like to say a small prayer request, such as:

Goddess Sulis, I call to thee
Join me please and lend your energy

Creating a Sulis Altar

Altars are very personal and should reflect you as a person as well as the deity you are honouring. Trust your intuition on what to place on the altar, also ask Sulis when you have made a connection with her, what would she like to see on the altar? Where you place your altar will often depend on what space you have in your home. An altar does not need to be large or grand, have a look around and see what spot feels right for you.

Altar placement suggestions:

> A dish – using a bowl or dish to place items into works well if you are tight on space, it can also be easily moved.
> A tray – creating an altar on a tray makes it moveable and it can be hidden away if necessary.
> Windowsill
> Sideboard
> Occasional table
> Inside a cupboard
> On a shelf
> Mantlepiece
> On a stone slab or piece of wood in the garden.
> Corner of your desk
> For Sulis having a small space on the windowsill in your bathroom works really well.

Again, what you place on your altar is entirely up to you, but here are my suggestions for items that I have on my own altar to Sulis or items I think connect well with her.

Do not be limited by thinking altar items need to be purchased from specialist occult shops. Anything goes! You can use ornaments, images printed from the internet, key rings, even children's toys. Be creative and have a look at what you already have in your home and keep an eye out in charity/thrift stores too. Artwork is wonderful for your altar, a lot of artists sell postcard or small size prints of their work for a reasonable price, do support them if you can.

Sun and Solar Symbols

- I have yet to find a statue specifically of Sulis, but you can find ornaments and figurines that you could use to represent her.

- Picture of the goddess, there are a few out there!
- Candles and holders, use colours that you associate with her.
- Representations of water such as shells or a dish of spring water.
- Images of the Roman Baths, if you ever get a chance to visit, they have a good gift shop.
- Image of the 'gorgon' head, you can print these from the internet but if you are lucky, you can sometimes find castings of it for sale by artisans. You could even create your own from modelling or air-dry clay.

Offering Dish

- Vase and fresh flowers, I like to put fresh flowers on all my altars, it brings a connection to nature and the seasons. You can also tie the choice of flowers to associate with the deity. For Sulis I like to have yellow and orange flowers and plenty of fresh herbs.
- I keep my tarot cards on my Sulis altar, as she is connected with divination skills.
- Coins – as so many of the offerings in the Bath springs are coins this seems fitting.
- The Sun tarot card.
- Pretty glass dishes and vases.
- Images or representations of owls, pigs or dolphins.
- Mosaic designs, the Romans loved their mosaic floors.

An altar cloth is useful to protect the surface underneath from candle wax but also to bring in some colour magic and it can be changed to represent the seasons too. Again, this need not be expensive, look out for scarves or shawls in charity/thrift stores or purchase 'fat quarters' of material from fabric stores.

Cleansing Your Altar

I like to cleanse and consecrate my sacred space regularly particularly if I am changing it for a new season or working with a different deity. I like to use blessed water to do this. Create your own blessed sacred water to use.

You will need:

Water
Sprigs of herbs such as rosemary, thyme or a piece of cinnamon
Clean jar or jug

You start with water (unsurprisingly), and it is your choice whether you use filtered, spring, tap water or collected rainwater. If you are worried about using tap water and all the icky stuff that is supposed to be in it, you can boil it first and allow it to cool.

Then you need to put it in a container, I find that a glass jar works very well. At this point if you feel the urge, you could charge and cleanse the water by holding your hand over the top and sending your intent into the water or you could waft some sage or incense over the top. Add in your sprigs of herbs.

You can charge your water under the moon, but for Sulis it feels right to use solar power. You can stand it out in the sunlight to capture the individual phases of the sun; sunrise, morning (waxing), midday (full), afternoon (waning) and sunset. Waxing and full bring in positive energy, waning and sunset release negative energy. Leave for at least an hour in your chosen phase, then it is ready for use.

To prepare your sacred space, physically clean the area with a duster or damp cloth to clean away any dust. Take your blessed water and sprinkle it over the area, in the four directions saying:

*To the east, with the blessings of the element of air, the season of
    spring and the maiden*
For intellect, intuition and inspiration
Make it so

*To the south, with the blessings of the element of fire, the season of
    summer and the mother*
For passion, creativity and energy
Make it so

*To the west, with the blessings of the element of water, the season
    of autumn and the matriarch*
For emotions, dreams and wishes
Make it so

*To the north, with the blessings of the element of earth, the season
    of winter and the crone*
For stability, grounding and love of hearth and home
Make it so

Then sprinkle some water in the centre of your space and say:

*In honour of the goddess Sulis, I cleanse and consecrate this as my
    sacred space.*
*Bringing together the elements of the seasons and the energy of
    the goddess.*
Make it so

Now adorn your space.

Offerings

I meditate regularly to meet with Sulis and each time I allow my
subconscious to decide what gifts I present to her. She seems to
like being presented with something on each visit. Generally,

the offerings tend to be of food, often grapes or fruit, sometimes cheese. Randomly on one occasion my brain instructed me to present her with a large platter of leeks, but Sulis seemed pleased. These offerings I give to her as visualisations in my meditations.

When I make physical offerings to Sulis I am often drawn to give copper coins, sometimes silver. I have several reproduction Roman coins that I also use. It seems fitting to me, but you must trust our own intuition. She also seems to like fresh herbs from my garden.

A suitable idea as an offering dish for Sulis is to have a bowl of spring water on your altar. You can drop coins, pretty stones or crystals into the water, as the offerings were made in the springs at Bath. When I was working with Sulis to help speed up our house renovation I put a dish on my altar filled with water and each day I put a few drops from a bottle of spring water I had purchased from the Roman Baths into it. As I added the spring water, I made my request. It was incredibly successful and Sulis moved everything along at the speed of light!

Here are some suggestions:

Coins
Herbs
Flowers
Food such as grapes or nuts
Shells or pebbles
Wine
Beads

I do not make offerings every day, although I do like to sit and light her candle and make a connection regularly. I do make offerings at least twice a week and particularly if I have made a request to her. It is a case of good manners, if you ask the goddess for something there must be an offering of thanks in some format.

When you make your offering remember to state what it is for. Charge the item with your intent by holding it in your hands and visualising your goal or desire or the reason you are giving it as an offering. Say something along the lines of:

Goddess Sulis, I ask you... (insert your request here) with my heartfelt thanks.

If you are just giving the item as an offering to honour Sulis you could say:

Goddess Sulis, I give this offering of (insert whatever it is here) as an honour to you and your continued support and guidance.

Finding Sulis

One of the most obvious ways to connect with Sulis is to bathe. Within Alan Richardson's excellent book, *Searching for Sulis* is an appendix written by Paul Dunne.[59] He suggests the best place to connect with Sulis is within your own home via the bath or shower, which is a genius idea! She is after all, a goddess of baths and bathing. You could even extend that to cover all the plumbing systems throughout the country.

Paul Dunne also suggests this idea,[60] which I find quite intriguing, it relates to the magical figure, Abaris, Master of The Hyperborean Mysteries:[61]

It is said the Hyperborean Mysteries have a secret home...which is in fact the British Isles. Abaris was the servant of the Hyperborean Apollo (Sun God) ...the linage of Abaris mirrors that of Bladdud.

It is also said that not only did Bladdud have the ability to fly, but he also started the Temple and Worship of the goddess Sulis at Bath.

He finishes up with the suggestion:

Bath itself represents the Magical Western Gate in the Lodge Temple of the British Mysteries and the Magical Energies of The Generative Powers of Great Britain. These powers and forces of Great Britain, or Old Albion, are brought to a head within the hot wellsprings of the Temple of Aqua Sulis.

Obviously just taking a bath or jumping in the shower is straightforward, but ritual bathing can be an amazing experience.

You could create a ritual bath to connect with the energy of Sulis, or if you like Dunne's idea, you might even treat it as a portal or gateway to Otherworlds. Springs and wells have been seen as this type of portal right back throughout history.

To create a ritual bath, I suggest using a nice bath bomb or bath salts that are scented with essential oils and include herbs of some kind. You can buy these from various places (I suggest purchasing from artisans and independent crafters) or you can have a go at making them yourself, I have given some basic recipes here:

Bath Salts
600g/21 oz sea salt
300g/10.5 oz Epsom salt
6 drops essential oil
1 teaspoon dried herbs or flower petals

Mix together and you have created your own bath salts. Sprinkle a few spoonfuls into your hot bath water.

Bath Melts
50g/2 oz shea butter
50g/2 oz cocoa butter
2 tablespoons coconut oil
20 drops essential oil

Put the shea and cocoa butter in a bowl over a pan of warm water. Leave them until the butters have melted together then add the coconut oil and the essential oils. Mix them to combine. Pour the mixture into soap moulds or small cupcake cases, you should get about ten of them out of this quantity. Leave to cool and set. Store the melts in the fridge, they will keep for up to three months.

Add a bath melt to your hot bath water. You can use them in the shower as a moisturiser.

If you do not want to make or purchase bath salts, bombs or melts then pop a few dried herbs into a small fabric pouch and hang it under the tap as you fill the bath.

Set the scene. It only takes a few minutes, but it really does make all the difference. If you are able to place tealights around the bath or at least a couple of candles on the bathroom windowsill safely, do it. It helps create a different mood for the occasion. This is not just you jumping in the shower or the bath for your daily ablutions this is something special. Put on some background music, something plinky plonky or even some Roman or Celtic style music might be fun (do a search on Spotify or YouTube). Light some incense or oil in a burner that corresponds to the goddess Sulis.

Once you are in the bath or shower, take your time. You want to honour the Goddess Sulis and even make a connection with her whilst you are there. Ask her to meet you or make contact with you.

Sulis Meditations

Sulis Roman Baths Meditation

One of the best and easiest ways to connect with Sulis, in fact with any deity, is by meditation. Set the scene that you believe is associated with Sulis, I have used the Roman Baths, but have also included an early time setting version as well.

Make yourself comfortable, close your eyes if you wish.

Focus on your breathing, deep breathes in...deep breathes out.

As your world around you dissipates you find yourself in a large courtyard, flat pale yellow stone slabs beneath your feet.

In front of you is a large imposing building with a set of stone steps leading up.

Above the steps are four large columns supporting a beautifully coloured pediment.

As your eyes draw you upwards you see a face in the stone on the top, eyes staring out from a circle of wild hair and beard. The face seems protective, as a guardian would be but also welcoming.

You walk forward and take the first step up, then the next, onto step 3, 4, 5, 6, 7, 8 and step 9.

Now you are standing between the columns facing a large wooden door.

It swings open inwards, and you step through.

You find yourself inside the temple with large flagstones across the floor and in the centre a stone altar. On each corner of the altar are figures carved into the stone.

Looking beyond the altar you see a gilded statue of a goddess glinting in the light thrown across the room by flaming torches on the walls.

She is a goddess, and you immediately know you are in the presence of the goddess Sulis.

Taking a look around you, there are raised platforms on either side of the room each one filled with bowls, dishes and trays full of fruits, vegetables and other produce.

Other dishes hold spices and herbs and one of them is full of hot coals that have been sprinkled with herbs and resins and you watch the scented smoke ascend upwards.

A further dish is filled with scented water, and you are moved to dip your hands in and wash them, breathing in the beautiful aroma as we do so.

Then you are drawn to pick up a tray and load it up with several items. These are your offerings to the goddess Sulis, trust your intuition and be guided by it to know what to choose for her.

With your tray filled with offerings you make your way to the centre of the room and the front of the altar.

Lay your offerings on the top of the stone altar.

Ask for blessings from the goddess and if you have a question now is the time to put it forward to her.

Listen carefully...

You may hear her voice, you might see images given by her or even just a feeling, pay attention to whatever comes your way.

When you are ready look up to the face of the statue and give your thanks to the goddess for her time, patience and wisdom.

Turn and make your way back out of the doorway and to the top of the stairs.

Take the first step down, then the next, step 7, 6, 5, 4, 3, 2 and step 1, back to the courtyard.

Give a last look up to the stone face on the pediment, he seems to smile back at you.

When you are ready, come back to the here and now.

Slowly and gently open your eyes, wriggle your fingers and toes.

Sulis Hot Springs Meditation

This version of a meditation to meet Sulis uses the setting of the hot springs, long before the Romans built the Baths over them.

Make yourself comfortable, close your eyes if you wish.

Focus on your breathing, deep breathes in...deep breathes out.

As your world around you dissipates you find yourself walking through trees, they are sparsely set, and you have plenty of forest floor to walk across between them. Take a look at the type of trees and notice the bark on the trunks and the leaves above you. As you walk you begin to see what looks like a hazy mist in front of you.

Keep walking towards it and you begin to detect a slight smell of sulphur in the air, a tang of bad eggs.

Stepping out from the tree line you find yourself in a field that is covered by a shroud of mist, but you realise it is actually steam coming from the ground.

As you move closer you begin to see pools of water which seem to be sourced from a spring underground.

Move yourself to the edge of one of the pools and put your hand down to touch the water. It is surprisingly warm, like that of a comforting bath.

As you are investigating you feel the presence of someone coming across the field.

Looking up you see a figure; it seems to be a woman. What colour hair does she have? What is she wearing?

She walks towards you and gives you a greeting which you return.

The woman tells you she is the goddess of these natural hot springs, and her name is Sulis.

She invites you to sit beside her and sooth your feet in the warm waters of the spring.

You make yourself comfortable and sitting down on the edge of one of the pools of water, you put your feet into the warmth of the hot spring waters.

Sulis sits beside you.

She asks if you have any questions for her of if there is anything she can help you with.

You talk with her...

Listen carefully to her response.

When you are ready you thank Sulis for her wisdom and stand up. She stands beside you and smiles, turning around and walking back off across the field.

You take a last look at the waters and the steam and turn, heading back towards the tree line.

Walking between the first trees you find yourself coming back to this reality.

Slowly and gently open your eyes, wriggle your fingers and toes.

Building a Relationship

What I cannot stress enough is how important it is to build a relationship with Sulis before asking her for things. In fact, this goes for any deity. The connection you have is built and earnt, it does not usually happen instantly. A relationship with deity is the same as any other, whether that is with your partner, friend or colleague, it will take time and effort to build and maintain. Keep making contact whether that is via meditation or prayer. Honour her with offerings and setting up an altar. Dedicate some of your time and energy to do things in her name, it might just be feeding the birds. You need to get to know her and her personality the same as she needs to get to know you. There are no short cuts to this or magic of any kind in fact.

Oaths

As we see from one of the tablets offered to the waters of Sulis she was seen as a figure of justice and judgement and obviously a deity that is suitable to make an oath in front of. This makes her perfect to call upon to witness any kind of oath, commitment or dedication. I have included a section in the ritual below which allows for this to be done, but you could certainly design your own ritual for that purpose. Make an oath to yourself for any reason such as more self-care or less pressure. An oath or dedication could be made to help you achieve your goals. A dedication could be made to the goddess as a promise that you will follow your spiritual pathway, whatever that might be. See it as a kind of self-initiation.

Sulis Ritual

In 2014 my coven, Kitchen Witch led a ritual in honour of Sulis, it was set in a grove of beech trees and surrounded by fields of grass.[62] Included within the ritual that day we also initiated several members into our coven, which is quite befitting of Sulis in her guise as an accepter of oaths. The ritual below is loosely based on that original one which was designed for a group, I have adapted it to be held as a solitary.

I use north, east, south and west as earth, air, fire and water, if this does not work for you, please do adapt it. I have also given a less ceremonial option for the circle casting at the end of the ritual if you prefer.

To make any ritual work properly and be successful requires your own energy and will. When you cast the circle really see and/or feel the sphere forming around you. As you call in each element visualise the properties of it, for example, when you call in fire, see flames in your mind's eye and feel the warmth on your skin. When you call in water visualise rivers and waves and feel the coolness of rain on your face. In ritual you are working with energy, so you need to really be on board and put some effort into it, otherwise you are just reading words that have no meaning.

You will need:

Flower petals, marigolds would be perfect
Small coins
Slips of paper and pen
Bowl of water

Four candles for the elements/quarters
A candle for Sulis
A candle for Belenus
Something to eat and drink

Begin by casting your circle, if you have the space to walk a circle that would be perfect, if not you can just turn around on the spot.

Sprinkle flower petals as you walk clockwise in a circle, visualise a protective circle forming around you, then see it rise up above you and down below, forming a sphere above, around you and below you. As you cast the circle say:

Sulis, goddess of power and might
Protect this circle and shine your light
Cast this circle round about
To keep energy in and the unwanted out
This circle is now cast

Turning to face the North and lighting the Earth candle, say:

Element of earth, I ask that you lend your magic of stability and grounding to this ritual, I welcome you.

Turning to face the East and lighting the Air candle, say:

Element of air, I ask that you lend your magic of intellect and wisdom to this ritual, I welcome you.

Turning to face the South and lighting the fire candle, say:

Element of fire, I ask that you lend your magic of creativity and passion to this ritual, I welcome you.

Turning to face the West and lighting the water candle, say:

Element of water, I ask that you lend your magic of emotions and flow to this ritual, I welcome you.

Face the centre and lighting the Sulis candle say:

Sulis, Lady of the sacred springs, I call upon you
Goddess of the sun and thermal waters
I ask you to bring your wisdom and power to this ritual
Join me and lend your blessings
I welcome you

Next light the Belenus candle and say:

Belenus, Lord of the Sun, light of the day, I call upon you
I ask you to bring your power and support to this ritual
Join me and lend your energy
I welcome you

Oath

If you have an oath or a pledge you would like to make do so at this point, it might be an oath to yourself or your own self-care. It could also be a pledge to dedicate yourself to your own spiritual pathway. Speak your words to the Goddess now.

Coin Wishes to Sulis

With the bowl filled with water in front of you along with the coins, slips of paper and pen this is the spell working part of the ritual.

Hold your hands over the bowl of water and say:

Mighty Sulis, Goddess of the eye to the Otherworld
I ask that you lend your magic to this working

Help me see between the veils
And guide me in my wishes

Now take a slip of paper and write your wish, goal or question on it.

Take one of the coins and wrap the paper around it.

Now drop the wrapped coin into the bowl of water.

You can repeat this as many times as you need.

When you are done, sit quietly and watch the water. Look for any symbols, listen for any sounds or messages. Use all your senses, keep them open and alert. Note how the paper and the coins react in the water too, this may have meaning. Spend some time with this.

When you are ready have a drink and a bite to eat. This will help ground you but also acknowledges that the Goddess provides for you. Keep a little drink and food to give as an offering to Sulis when you have finished the ritual. This can be tipped on the ground.

Now you can close the ritual down.

Facing the centre, say:

Sulis, Lady of the sacred springs, I thank you for your energy here today.
Stay if you will, go if you must, with my heartfelt thanks.

Snuff out the Sulis candle.

Belenus, Lord of the Sun, I thank you for your energy here today.
Stay if you will, go if you must, with my heartfelt thanks.

Snuff out the Belenus candle.

Turn to face the West, say:

Element of water I thank you for your energy here today.

Snuff out the water candle.

Turn to face the South, say:

Element of fire I thank you for your energy here today.

Snuff out the fire candle.

Turn to face the East, say:

Element of air I thank you for your energy here today.

Snuff out the air candle.

Turn to face the North, say:

Element of earth I thank you for your energy here today.

Snuff out the earth candle.

Now close the circle, walking anti clockwise. If you sprinkled petals on the ground to cast the circle, you could sweep these up as you walk, or if you are outside, they can be left. Visualise the sphere dissipating as you walk. Say:

Sulis, Goddess of power and might
Release this circle, but keep the light
This circle is now uncast
But may the strength and protection last

The water from the bowl can be poured onto the garden. The paper can be put in the compost or trash. The coins can either be placed on your altar as a reminder or buried. Trust your intuition as to what you need to do with them.

Options

If you prefer a less structured and ceremonial ritual, you can just work the spell or oath without casting a circle or calling in the quarters. I would recommend lighting the candle to Sulis though and calling in her energies.

Another way to work with ritual, one that we do in our Kitchen Witch coven is below, instead of casting the circle and calling the quarters. My thanks to Ness, Sue and Heather for these alternatives.

Hand to Heart Method

We will connect to our sacred space.

Take three long deep breaths.

Standing or sitting, with both hands on your heart and say, "from my heart", stretching both hands into the air, say "to the sky".

Putting both hands on or facing down to the earth, as close to it as you can get, say "to the land".

Putting both hands on your heart, say "to my heart".

Leaving both hands on your heart, say "from my heart", reaching out your right hand, "to all points on the compass".

Reach out your left hand and place your right hand on your heart and say, "to all directions".

Putting both hands on your heart, say "to my heart".

Visualisation Method

This is a short visualisation to bring us together in ritual and to connect with the elements.

Sit comfortably, close your eyes and take 3 deep breaths in... and slowly exhale out...

Picture yourself walking along a woodland path. In the azure sky above, the sun is warm and bright and there is not a cloud in sight. The sunlight peeks its way through the surrounding trees. Your footpath is lined with flowers, trees and plants. You follow the footpath to a clearing where an ancient moss and lichen covered stone wall trails around the grassy landscape.

You become aware of others standing with you – some faces you recognise, others are new, but you know that everyone is here for the same reason – to honour and join you in ritual.

As you stand in the clearing, you become aware of the lush green grasses beneath your feet – it is soft and warm against your feet – we welcome Earth.

Running along the edge of the path is a small stream, its waters cold and crystal clear – we welcome Water.

A soft warm breeze brushes against your hair and making the grasses in the clearing where you stand dance delightfully – we welcome Air.

Some of the people around you are holding lit candles of reds, oranges and yellows – we welcome Fire.

When you are ready, open your eyes.

Either of these work in place of casting the circle and calling the quarters as I have laid out in the formal ritual. Once you have done this you would then move onto the spell working part of your ritual.

To close down:

Hand to Heart Method
To disconnect from your sacred space.

Standing or sitting, with both hands on your heart and say, "from my heart", stretching both hands into the air, say "to the sky".

Putting both hands on or facing down to the earth, as close to it as you can get, say "to the land".

Putting both hands on your heart, say "to my heart".

Leaving both hands on your heart, say "from my heart", reaching out your right hand, "from all points of the compass".

Reach out your left hand and place your right hand on your heart and say, "from all directions".

Both hands on your heart, say "to my heart, thank you".

Visualisation Method

Take a few deep breaths. Close your eyes and take yourself back to the clearing beside the woodland path. We are honoured to have been a part of this ritual. Take a look around you, the sun is lower in the sky now, but it is still warm. The people that you were with are dispersing back down the woodland pathway. Take a moment to thank the elements and the land that we have stood upon, then when you are ready, come back to this reality.

Herbals

I have based some of my choices on the solar energy that Sulis carries and use herbals that correspond to the intents that you would call upon her for.[63] Others included here are because the ancient Romans were responsible for introducing them to Britain or they were popular in ancient Rome for their gardens or ceremonies. I have also drawn inspiration from foods and plants that the ancient people of Britain would have had access to. These are just my suggestions, trust your intuition and what resonates with you.

These herbs, plants and spices can be used as offerings, to create incense or essential oil blends or used in spell work that calls upon the energy of Sulis. Add them to your spell pouches, witch bottles or dress your candles and create sachet powders with them.

Barley – One of the first grains ancient Britons would have eaten, mixed with wheat and roasted over a fire to create a type of bread. Barley is ruled by Venus and the element of earth, it brings the magic of healing, grounding and protection.

Bay – A fiery plant, native to Britain and ruled by the sun. The bay was a scared herb for the Romans and symbolised peace, prophecy and victory. Bay brings the magic of creativity, healing, power, psychic powers, purification, spirituality and strength.

Black pepper – A fiery spice that is ruled by Mars and brings the magic of confidence and strength but is used to protect against or remove jealousy, gossip and negative energy.

Blackthorn – A fiery plant ruled by Saturn and Mars and brings the magic of divination and healing. It can also be used to exorcise negative energy and bring in protection.

Cedar – Ruled by the Sun and Jupiter and a fire element plant, cedar brings the magic of the Goddess as a whole but also brings in purification and protection.

Cinnamon – A very useful magical spice that brings the energy of the Sun and the element of fire. Cinnamon has the magical properties of dealing with changes, focus, healing, power, psychic abilities, protection and success. It was also a spice used by the Romans.

Cloves – They pack a huge punch of fire energy and are ruled by Jupiter. They bring in the magic of abundance, clarity, exorcising negative energy, preventing gossip and finding the truth. Cloves were highly valued by the Romans and were very expensive.

Fennel – Introduced to Britain by the Romans, fennel was given to gladiators to increase their strength and stamina. Fennel is ruled by Mercury and the element of fire. It brings the magic of healing, purification and protection.

Frankincense – A tree resin used by the Romans in their incense blends. It is ruled by the Sun and the element of fire. Frankincense brings the magic of abundance, focus, spirituality and purification.

Grapes – Perhaps one of the most recognised fruits associated with ancient Rome is the grape. The Romans brought grapes over to Britain with them and they can be successfully grown here. Grapes are ruled by the Moon and are both an air and water element. Grapes bring the magic of fertility and spirituality; they also make excellent offerings to deity (as does the wine that is made from them).

Hazelnuts – The hazelnut is ruled by the Sun and Mercury and the element of air. Hazelnuts would have been a good source of food in ancient Britain. Hazelnut brings the magic of healing, fertility, psychic powers, protection and wisdom.

Juniper – Dating back to Neolithic times, apparently, Juniper is ruled by the Sun, Jupiter and the Moon and aligns with the element of fire. Juniper brings the magic clarity, exorcising negative energy, justice, psychic powers, stolen items, healing, purification and protection.

Lavender – Native to Britain the lavender plant also appears in a lot of formal Roman gardens. Ruled by Mercury and an air element, lavender brings the magic of clarity, happiness, protection and strength.

Marigold – The Romans introduced the marigold flower to Britain. Marigold is ruled by the Sun and the element of fire. Marigold brings the magic of happiness, dispelling gossip, psychic powers and protection.

Marjoram/Oregano – Native to Britain, but variations can be found across Europe and Asia. The ancient Romans (and Greeks) used marjoram for the magical purpose of love and happiness. It is ruled by Mercury and the element of air and brings the magic of good health and protection.

Myrrh – In ancient Rome myrrh resin was used in incense blends and as an oil for rituals. Myrrh is ruled by the Sun and Mars and the element of water. Myrrh brings the magic of courage, healing, protection, purification and as a connection to the Underworld.

Nettles – The humble nettle is ruled by Mars and the element of fire. The nettle would have been used and eaten in ancient Britain. Nettle brings the magic of healing exorcising negative energy, money and protection.

Olives – I have included olives here, because I use it in the form of olive oil to fill the terracotta oil lamps that the Romans used. It is also a good oil to use for anointing and as a base for essential oil blends. Olive is ruled by the sun and is a fire and air element. Olive brings the magic of integrity, healing, fertility, passion, peace, spirituality, luck and protection.

Rose – A recognised flower in a lot of English gardens, but the rose can be found across the globe. Wild roses are native to Britain though. The Romans loved roses and used them in bathing, celebration, decoration and seduction. Rose is ruled by Venus and the Moon and the element of water. Rose brings the magic of abundance, death and rebirth, healing, knowledge, love and psychic powers.

Rosemary – Ruled by the Sun and the element of fire. It was introduced to Britain by the Romans and used in crowns and garlands for knowledge and good memory. Rosemary brings the magic of exorcising negative energy, healing, protection and purification.

Thyme – Introduced to Britain by the Romans, the oil of which was used for massage and added to baths to increase energy. Thyme is ruled by Venus and is a water element herb, bringing the magic of courage, healing and good health, peace, psychic powers, purification and release.

Sulis – Loose Incense Mix
Equal parts:

> Frankincense
> Rosemary
> Cloves

Sulis – Oil Blend
Oil blends can be used to anoint yourself before ritual, added to your bathwater, used for aromatherapy, burning in an oil burner or used to dress candles. Never put essential oil directly onto your skin, always mix with a base oil first.

> 10ml olive oil
> 10 drops rose essential oil
> 10 drops myrrh essential oil
> 5 drops cinnamon essential oil

Crystals

Crystals are frequently used in modern Witchcraft, and they correspond quite well with Sulis and the offerings of gemstones that were made to her. You do not need to spend a lot of money, tumble stones are small polished crystals which are usually inexpensive and are perfectly good to work with, in fact I prefer working with them for spells. Tumble stones can also be used on your altar and as offerings to Sulis. When you have finished working with them, they can be cleansed and used again. My choices are based on gemstones that were found in the springs at Bath with the addition of crystals I feel have a strong association with Sulis. Here are my suggestions, but as always trust your intuition and be guided by which ones you are drawn to:[64]

Amber – This fossilised resin is pure liquid sunshine, ruled by the Sun and the elements of fire and spirit. It is incredibly ancient and was apparently one of the first items worn as jewellery. Amber brings the magic of energy, solar magic, wishes, clarity, wisdom, psychic abilities, healing, abundance, cleansing and creativity.

Amethyst – This stone is a good all-rounder for lots of magical intents. It was one of the stones included in the carved gemstones that were found in the springs at Bath. Amethyst is ruled by Jupiter and Neptune and the element of water. Amethyst brings the magic of protection, hidden knowledge, transformation, breaking patterns, judgement, clarity, justice and focus.

Black Obsidian – This crystal is formed from volcanic lava, so it carries the energy of the elements of fire, earth and water. It is ruled by Saturn and Jupiter. Black obsidian brings the magic of truth, healing, clarity, strength, courage, protection, cleansing, focus, power, releasing, spirit work and divination.

Bloodstone – Bloodstone has such a powerful name and reminds me of sacrifices. Bloodstone is sometimes called heliotrope which translates from Greek to mean 'sun to turn'. Bloodstone is ruled by Mars and the elements of fire and earth. It brings the magic of clarity, energy, confidence, protection, insight, truth, intuition, creativity, strength, healing and divine connection.

Carnelian – A fire element crystal ruled by the Sun, carnelian brings in the magic of protection, confidence, success, courage, creativity, motivation, passion, truth, honesty, trust and abundance. Carnelian was one of the stones included in the carved gemstones that were found in the springs at Bath.

Citrine – Citrine is ruled by the Sun and Jupiter and the element of fire. In ancient Rome it was used as a talisman against evil. Citrine brings the magic of dispelling negative energy, solar magic, abundance, intuition, healing, creativity, confidence, protection, psychic powers and clarity.

Pyrite – or as it is commonly known, 'fool's gold'. The name pyrite comes from the Greek word 'pry' which translates as 'fire'. Pyrite has been used throughout history for healing and sometimes polished and used for divination. Pyrite is ruled by the Sun and Mars and the element of fire, it brings the magic of releasing, clarity, protection, inspiration, perception, wisdom, psychic abilities, healing, cleansing, abundance, strength, motivation, solar magic, energy, focus, divination and confidence.

Red Jasper – Red Jasper is a fire element stone ruled by Mars and brings in the magic of health, healing, protection, transformation and dispelling negative energy. Red Jasper was one of the stones included in the carved gemstones that were found in the springs at Bath.

Serpentine – Romans used serpentine as a protection against dark magic, it was also thought to break if it came in contact with poison. Serpentine is ruled by Saturn and the element of fire. Serpentine brings the magic of clarity, protection, dispels negative energy, psychic protection and cleansing.

Sunstone – This crystal is ruled by the Sun and the element of fire. Sunstone brings the magic of power, solar magic, strength, inspiration, clarity, intuition, confidence, healing, abundance and protection.

Animals

In most myths and legends of deities they are often associated with some kind of animal. Whilst we do not know for sure if Sulis had specific animals in her stories, we can make a guess and work with the animals that might have been.

Pigs and Wild Boar

With the story of Bladud we get the connection with pigs. I am taking this a step further to include wild boar which would have been native and plentiful in ancient Briton. I wonder as well whether the term 'pig' may have originally covered many types. The term 'boar' is used in farming to denote a male pig, but the widely used term 'wild boar' covers male and female. Swine of all types come from a common ancestor, the Eurasian wild boar or Sus scrofa. Wild boars are of the Sus scrofa species, but the domestic pig is a subspecies, the Sus scrofa domesticus. We began domesticating the 'wild pig' sometime around 8000 BC. Were Bladud's pigs of the domestic type or the wild ones? Anyway...enough hog talk. The connection with Bladud leads me to associate swine with Sulis. Not just because my main animal guide of many years is a boar! The boar carries a strong warrior energy who brings strength, transformation, protection, truth and power.

Owl

Owl comes in with the Minerva connection to Sulis. I think it sits quite well as some species of owl are native to Britain and have been for thousands of years. Owls have always had a strong connection to the Otherworld and appear in many myths and legends. The owl brings the magic of protection, death and rebirth, uncovering deception, wisdom, secrets and magic of all kinds.

Dolphin

Dolphin is a tricky one, and I think this is a direct influence from the Romans. Britain does have dolphins along some of the coastal areas now. I could not find any evidence of them in ancient times although some sources state the ancient Celts associated dolphins with sea deities.[65] The Romans, however, loved dolphins and they feature in a lot of their mosaics and decorations. Does the dolphin fit with Sulis? Personally, I do not associate her with them, but you might, their magical properties certainly fit with her though. Dolphin brings the magic of healing, balance, wisdom and all kinds of water magic.

Fish and Birds

A brooch was found in the springs, potentially given as an offering, which had images of a bird head and a fish. Experts have wondered whether the bird and fish were symbols of Sulis, perhaps from a long-forgotten legend or were they were just decorations on the brooch? Neither seem to fit Sulis in my opinion. She is associated with water obviously, but the springs are naturally hot, and I do not believe fish would be able to live in it. Is the connection with birds more probable? The ancient Celts did seem to have an affinity with birds and fish, and they honoured the spirits of many animals.[66] Birds had a strong connection with the Otherworld. The blackbird in particular is associated with the Otherworld, spirituality, healing and meditation. The salmon brings the magic of wisdom and knowledge and features in several ancient Celtic myths.

Divination

Sulis is a goddess of divination, all seeing and all-knowing with a view into the Otherworld. She can be called upon to help with divination and psychic skills of all kinds. She can lend her energy to all the regular divination tools such as tarot, oracle cards, pendulum and the crystal ball but I think she lends herself to water scrying particularly well. I call upon her for all types of readings and to boost my psychic abilities and connection.

Water Scrying

Water scrying is easy to set up, you will need a dish preferably with a darker interior as it helps with the reflections. Fill the dish with water and you have a water scrying dish. It helps if you light a candle and allow the flame to reflect on the surface of the water. I find adding a silver coin to the bottom of the dish aids too. You can sprinkle a pinch of dried herbs on the water or a few drops of ink. This all helps to provide images and shapes on the surface of the water.

Call upon the energy and wisdom of Sulis to help you in your reading. You could use a request such as:

Goddess Sulis, I ask for your wisdom and sight
To help me divine the answers to my questions this night

I like to light my Sulis candle at this point too. Now relax and ask your question. Gaze across the surface of the water and see what images or symbols you can find, open all your senses and listen for messages too.

Lithomancy

Lithomancy is the name for a set of stones which you throw and determine what they mean and where they lay. It is an old form of divination and brings in your personal energy with the items that you choose for your lithomancy set. It is also a less gruesome form of divination than reading entrails.

You will need a set of small items such as pebbles, shells, seed heads, small bones and/or crystal tumble stones. I like to use a mixture of items, but you can make a set just from one.

About ten small items in total works well. You can just shake the items between your hands and throw them on a flat surface and allow your intuition to work, reading any patterns or designs you see.

Another option is to designate each small item to a particular meaning. You might have a brown pebble and decide that represents the home or stability. A shell could relate to emotions and a small bone to the ancestors. A heart shaped crystal might be the representation for love matters and a silver coin could be money issues. You would then cast the items on a flat surface and read where each of them fell. Closer together might mean the meanings relate to each other, further away from the centre of your reading and those matters are less important.

A set made purely from crystals could be designed using their general meanings, for example, a piece of rose quartz might indicate love matters and a piece of green aventurine would be finances. Lithomancy sets are very personal and can be designed to your own specifications.

Call upon Sulis before you begin your reading and ask for her assistance.

Flames and Smoke Divination

The Haruspex from ancient times may also have read flames and smoke from the ritual fires. You can do this using just a candle to use the flame or incense to read the smoke. If you have a fire pit, open fire or chiminea you can read the flames, the smoke and the ash. Sit quietly in front of your source and ask a question, calling upon the insight of Sulis to aid you. Watch the flames and/or the smoke and look for any images and symbols. Open up all your senses, listen for any messages that you may receive as well.

Petitions

When making requests to Sulis, petitions are a fitting method to use. This seems to reflect the curse tablets that were found in her spring, each one written on a piece of pewter and folded before offering it up to her. Getting hold of sheets of pewter and etching your request is a little difficult so I tend to write petitions on slips of paper and place them in a dish of water on my altar. When I was last in Bath, I purchased a bottle of the spring water, so I add a few drops from that to each new offering dish of water and I regularly bless my altar to her with the water from the springs.

If you like the idea of a pewter type of petition, there is an easier alternative. You will need a piece of aluminium foil, yep, the regular stuff you use in the kitchen. Tear off a piece in a rectangular shape. Then you write your petition request onto the foil, I have found that a slightly blunt pencil works best, pens are too sharp.

Make sure to include 'To the Goddess Sulis' and give your vow to her. The foil can then be folded and dropped into a dish of water or pinned above your altar. Leave it in place until the request is granted, or you feel it is finished with. Dispose of the foil in the recycling waste.

Curses

Sulis seems to have been a 'go to' goddess for curse requests, with the amount of curse tablets found she must have been sought out regularly for justice. I am not going to judge anyone for wanting to put a request in for a curse, that decision is one that only you can make. But I do want to put some thoughts here about cursing, not to sway anyone, just my own viewpoint, you can take it or leave it. If you are angry with someone, stop and think about it first before hurling out a curse. Spells of any kind worked in anger have a nasty habit of going off in unexpected directions. Calm down first, then think about your course of action. Some situations may warrant action or reaction, but it is not always easy to decide what course to take. Never take the act of casting a curse lightly, in fact that really is good advice for any spell work. When you create a spell whether it is a positive or negative one, you are manipulating energy and that energy will affect someone. Take responsibility for all your spell work. A curse is defined as 'the wilful direction of negative energy towards someone with the intent to harm'.[67] If that is your goal, then have at it, just make sure you have crafted the curse carefully, you do not want to be dealing with the backlash.

Recipes

I love food and I find that researching, creating and eating food that has an association to the area that a deity comes from can help make a connection to them. I tend to stick with desserts and baked goods as they work well to use for feasting in group or solitary ritual. Breads and baked goods also work well to give a little of as offerings. Add to that my love of baking, of course! Here are some of my suggested recipes.

Celtic Sweet Bean Cakes

The ancient Celts would have eaten simple foods, meat, fish, bread, butter and cheese, they also had vegetable crops such as beans and peas and foraged leaves.[68]

250g/9 oz butter

500g/17 1.2 oz whole wheat flour

500g/17 ½ oz Celtic beans (Celtic bean (Vicia faba L.), broad/
fava bean), blanched

500g/17 ½ oz honey

125g/4 ½ oz chopped hazelnuts

Rub the butter into the flour until it resembles the texture of breadcrumbs. Mash the beans and add them to the flour mixture. Stir in the honey and hazelnuts. Drop spoonfuls of the mixture onto a hot griddle or pan, cook until each side is light brown.

Roman Patina

This is essentially an omelette which is turned out onto a plate and cut into wedges to serve.[69] The recipe includes fish sauce, which the Romans used in lots of dishes, you can omit it, but the flavour will not be the same obviously!

30g/1 oz flaked almonds

30g/1 oz hazelnuts

30g/1 oz pine kernels

Black pepper

40ml/1 ½ fl oz milk

40ml/1 ½ fl oz white wine

1 tablespoon honey plus extra for drizzling

1 tablespoon fish sauce

4 eggs

1 tablespoon olive oil

Mix the nuts together and toast them until lightly brown. Whizz them in a processor until they are a coarse ground texture. Mix them together with the pepper, milk, wine, honey, fish sauce and eggs. Warm the oil in a pan and pour in the mixture, cook over a medium heat until nicely set. Turn out and pour over a little honey to serve.

Bath Buns

Dating back to the 18th Century, the Bath bun was eaten by the wealthy people once they had visited the healing waters from the natural spring in Bath, Somerset.[70]

> 1 teaspoon salt
> 450g/1 lb strong white bread flour
> 4 teaspoons dried fast action yeast
> 150ml/1/4 pint warm milk
> 60ml/4 tablespoons warm water
> 50g/2 oz caster sugar
> 2 eggs
> 50g/2 oz butter, melted and cooled
> 170g/6 oz sultanas
> 25g/1 oz mixed peel
> Beaten egg and caster sugar to top

Line two baking sheets.

Mix the yeast, milk and water with 100g/3 ½ oz of the flour. Leave in a warm place for ten minutes until the mixture is frothy.

Pop the remaining flour and salt into a bowl and add the sugar.

Stir in the eggs, butter, yeast mixture, sultanas and peel. Mix to combine, it will be a wet sticky dough.

Turn onto a floured board and knead for 5-10 minutes until smooth.

Pop the dough into a bowl and cover.

Leave to rise in a warm place for 1-2 hours, until doubled in size.

Give the dough a mix and knock back the air. It will be sticky.

Place spoonfuls onto the prepared baking sheets – you can get 12 to 16 buns.

Cover with a cloth and leave in a warm place for 45 minutes to rise again.

Then brush the tops with beaten egg and sprinkle with sugar.

Preheat your oven to 375F/190C/Gas 5.

Bake for 15 minutes until light golden brown.

Serve split and buttered.

Sally Lunns

Although this recipe is not as old as the origins of Sulis, it has strong connections and is just around the corner from the Roman Baths. The Sally Lunn Eating House is one of the oldest buildings in the city of Bath, Somerset.[71] Although it sits in its present form dating back to 1925 the origins of the Sally Lunn bun go back to the mid/late 1600s. Legend says that Sally Lunn was a French Huguenot lady who arrived in Britain in 1680. She worked in a Bath bakery and introduced her French breakfast cake. I have eaten in the Sally Lunn Eating House; it is a fascinating building. I have had Sally Lunn's split and spread with cinnamon butter there and also a beef casserole served on top of a Sally Lunn.

1 teaspoon salt

50g/2 oz butter

200ml/7 fl oz milk

1 teaspoon caster sugar

7g/2 ¼ teaspoons fast action dried yeast

2 eggs

450g/1lb strong white bread flour

Melt the butter and add in the milk and sugar. Stir well.

Add the yeast and the eggs, mix together.

Pop the flour and salt into a large bowl and then add the milk and yeast mixture.

Mix well and knead lightly for a few minutes.

Grease two 5"/13 cm cake tins.

I chose to use individual Yorkshire pudding tins as that's what I have, they are smaller (about 3 ½" in diameter) so I split the dough into four rather than two. If you use smaller tins your buns will be deeper than the traditional slightly flatter, wider Sally Lunn.

Divide the dough into two and shape into rounds, put them in the 5" tins and cover with a cloth.

Leave in a warm place to rise, around 45 minutes.

Preheat your oven to 450F/230C/Gas 8.

Bake the Sally Lunns for about 15-20 minutes.

Once the buns are cooked you can glaze them with a mixture of 2 tablespoons sugar dissolved in two tablespoons water, brush on whilst warm.

Sally Lunns are traditionally served split in half with butter or cream. Cinnamon butter is really nice, just mix some ground cinnamon with butter. Or you can use them with just butter for eating with soup or savoury dishes.

The Final Problem

Part of the problem with the Roman Baths is the ability to do any further serious archaeological work. Although today we can see a lovely stone building that surrounds the main bath, a huge amount of the remains are under the ground. And that ground is covered by a cathedral and surrounding shops and buildings. Not so easy to dismantle a cathedral just to be able to dig up a temple! However, work does continue in as much as they can, new discoveries are often made to help us understand the story of the Baths. The other point to note is that most of the work has been done to unearth and study the Baths themselves, any delving into the goddess has been sidelined somewhat. Of course, the question is, how much more information could we find on her? There do not appear to be any local myths or legends about her, no stories were told around the fire on late winter nights about her escapades. Perhaps that is part of what draws me to her, the mystery and the unknown and the knowledge that my journey with her is very personal. Yours will be too.

Endnotes

1   *The Waters of the Gap,* Bob Stewart
2   Gaius Julius Solinus - *De Mirabilis Mundi* - Translation by Arwen Apps - 2011
3   *Historia Brittonum,* 9th Century
4   *Roman Bath,* Peter Davenport, 2021
5   Itinerarium Provinciarum Antoni(ni) Augusti – a list of stopping places along various Roman roads across their Empire – est. circa AD 107-AD 284
6   Ptolemy, 2nd Century
7   *Roman Bath,* Peter Davenport, 2021
8   *Searching for Sulis,* Alan Richardson & Margaret Haffenden, 2019
9   *Searching for Sulis,* Alan Richardson & Margaret Haffenden, 2019
10 *The Waters of the Gap,* Bob Stewart
11. *An Imperial Image: The Bath Gorgon in Context,* Eleri H. Cousins, 2016
12 *An Imperial Image: The Bath Gorgon in Context,* Eleri H. Cousins, 2016
13 *An Imperial Image: The Bath Gorgon in Context,* Eleri H. Cousins, 2016
14 https://penelope.uchicago.edu/
15 www.britannica.com
16 www.theoi.com
17 *Britannia AM,* Cousins, 2016
18 *Gods & Goddesses of England,* Rachel Patterson, 2023
19 *Roman Bath Discovered,* Barry Cunliffe, 1984
20 *Roman Bath,* Barry Cunliffe, 1995
21 www.romaninscriptionsofbritain.org
22 https://pleiades.stoa.org/
23 https://www.roman-britain.co.uk/

24 https://www.roman-britain.co.uk/

25 *Dictionary of Roman Religion*, L Adkins & R Adkins, 1196

26 *Roman Bath Discovered*, Barry Cunliffe, 1984

27 *Roman Bath*, Peter Davenport, 2021

28 *The Roman Curse Tablets from the Bath*, Fahimeh Rahraven

29 *Curses from the Waters of Sulis*, Dan R Jordan

30 *Voices from the sacred spring*, Roger Tomlin, 1992

31 Latin Dictionary & Grammar resources, Kevin D Mahoney

32 Roger Tomlin

33. Denoting or relating to the southern group of Celtic languages, consisting of Welsh, Cornish, and Breton. They were spoken in Britain before and during the Roman occupation, surviving as Welsh and Cornish after the Anglo-Saxon invasions (Oxford dictionary)

34 Philip Kiernan, Roger Tomlin, Stuart, Mckie

35 https://romaninscriptionsofbritain.org/

36 *Curse Tablets and Binding spells from the ancient world*, John G Gager, 1999

37 *The Curse Tablets Temple of Sulis Minerva*, Tomlin

38 Etruscan, member of an ancient people of Etruria, Italy, between the Tiber and Arno rivers west and south of the Apennines, whose urban civilization reached its height in the 6th century BC – Britannica.com

39 *Merriam Webster* dictionary

40 Geoffrey of Monmouth's *Historia Regum Britanniae* (The History of the Kings of Britain) circa 1136 AD

41 Geoffrey of Monmouth – *History of the Kings of Britain* – translated by Aaron Thompson with revisions by J. A. Giles

42 *Chronicle of the Early Britons*, Wm R Cooper

43 *Thermae redivivae*, Henry Chapman, 1673

44 Langtoft, Peter of. 'A Fool's Bolt soon Shott at Stonage'. In *Peter Langtoft's Chronicle*, 2vols. 1725

45 *The Waters of the Gap*, Bob Stewart

46 *Dictionary of Roman Religion*, L Adkins & Roy Adkins 1996

47 *Religio Romana Handbook,* L. Vitellius Triarius, 2014

48 *Sulis Rising,* Paul Dunne

49 *The Waters of the Gap,* Bob Stewart

50 *The Waters of the Gap,* Bob Stewart

51 *Holy Wells of Bath & Bristol Region,* Phil Quinn

52 *The Waters of the Gap,* Bob Stewart

53 *Pagan Celtic Britain,* Dr Anne Ross

54 *Roman Bath Discovered,* Barry Cunliffe, 1984

55 Ex voto – An object left as an offering in fulfilment of a vow or in gratitude, as recovery from an illness or injury

56 *Roman Bath Discovered,* Barry Cunliffe, 1984

57 *The Torch of Brighid,* Erin Aurelia, 2023

58 *Dictionary of Roman Religion,* L Adkins & R Adkins, 1996

59 *Searching for Sulis,* Alan Richardson & Margaret Haffenden, 2019

60 *Searching for Sulis,* Alan Richardson & Margaret Haffenden, 2019

61 https://www.worldhistory.org/Hyperborea

62 www.kitchenwitchhearth.net

63 *A Kitchen Witch's Guide to Magical Plants and Herbs,* and *A Kitchen Witch's Guide to Magical Food,* Rachel Patterson, 2014 & 2015 and RHS.org.uk/historicherbs

64 *Kitchen Witchcraft Series, Crystal Magic* Patterson, R

65 https://www.roman-britain.co.uk/

66 https://www.roman-britain.co.uk/

67 *Kitchen Witchcraft Series, Spells & Charms,* Patterson R

68 *Tasting the Past,* Jacqui Wood, 2009

69 Cooking Apicius, Sally Grainger, 2006

70 www.thebathbun.com

71 www.sallylunns.co.uk

Recommended Further Reading

Cunliffe, Barry – *Roman Bath* (1995)

Cunliffe, Barry – *Roman Bath Discovered* (1984)

Davenport, Peter – *Roman Bath* (2021)

Gager, John G – *Curse Tablets and Binding Spells from the Ancient World* (1999)

Green, Miranda – *The Gods of the Celts* (1986)

Green, Miranda – *Sacred Britannia* (2018)

Jordan, Dan R – *Curses from the Waters of Sulis* (1988)

Pierce, Robert – *The History And Memoirs Of The Bath: Containing Observations On What Cures Have Been There Wrought, Both By Bathing And Drinking Those Waters* (1713)

Quinn, Phil – *Holy Wells of Bath & Bristol Region* (1999)

Richardson, Alan/Haffenden, Margaret – *Searching for Sulis* (2019)

Ross, Anne, Dr – *Pagan Celtic Britain* (1992)

Savage, Anne (editor) – *The Anglo-Saxon Chronicles* (1996)

Stewart, Bob – *The Waters of the Gap* (1981)

Tomlin, Roger – *Voices from the Spring* (1992)

Academic Papers

Adams, J - British Latin: The Text, Interpretation and Language of the Bath Curse Tablets (1992)

Bruun, Christer – Lotores: Roman Bath Attendants (1993)

Cooper, Bill – The Chronical of the Early Britons

Cousins, Eleri H – An Imperial Image: The Bath Gorgon in Context (2016)

Gerrard, James - The Temple of Sulis Minerva at Bath and the End of Roman Britain (2008)

Irby, George – Military Religion in Roman Britain (2018)

Preston, Abigail – Roman Law and Magic (2021)

Rahraven, Fahimeh – The Roman Curse Tablets from the Bath Manuscripts for Religion and Magic (2022)

Stern, Tiffany – Bath and Bladud: The progress of a wayward myth (2021)

Sullivan, Ryan – Striking the Sacred: Religious Imagery on British Iron Age Coins (2010)

Visit

www.romanbaths.co.uk

www.thenovium.org

www.sussexpast.co.uk/attraction/fishbourne-roman-palace

About the Author

I am an English witch who has been walking the Pagan pathway for over thirty years. A working wife and mother who has been lucky enough to have had over 25 books published (so far), some of them becoming best sellers. My passion is to learn, I love to study and have done so from books, online resources, schools and wonderful mentors over the years and still continue to learn each and every day, but I have learnt the most from actually getting outside and doing it.

I like to laugh ... and eat cake...

It is my pleasure to give talks to pagan groups and co-run open rituals and workshops run by the Kitchen Witch Coven. I am also High Priestess of the Kitchen Witch Coven and an Elder at the online Kitchen Witch School of Natural Witchcraft.

A regular columnist with Fate & Fortune magazine, I also contribute articles to several magazines such as Pagan Dawn and Witchcraft & Wicca. You will find my regular ramblings on my own personal blog and YouTube channel.

My craft is a combination of old religion witchcraft, Wicca, hedge witchery, kitchen witchery and folk magic. My heart is that of an English Kitchen Witch.

It was my honour to be added to the Watkins 'Spiritual 100 List' for 2023.

Special thanks to the artist Suzi Edwards Goose (The Ink Witch) for creating the image of Sulis for the front cover.

www.rachelpatterson.co.uk
facebook.com/rachelpattersonbooks
www.kitchenwitchhearth.net
facebook.com/kitchenwitchuk
Email: HQ@kitchenwitchhearth.net
www.youtube.com/user/Kitchenwitchuk
www.instagram.com/racheltansypatterson

MY BOOKS

Kitchen Witchcraft Series
Spells & Charms
Garden Magic
Crystal Magic
The Element of Earth
The Element of Fire
The Element of Water

Pagan Portals
Kitchen Witchcraft
Hoodoo Folk Magic
Moon Magic
Meditation
The Cailleach
Animal Magic
Sun Magic
Triple Goddess
Gods & Goddesses of England
Dragon Magic

Other Moon Books

The Art of Ritual
Beneath the Moon
Witchcraft … into the Wilds
Grimoire of a Kitchen Witch
A Kitchen Witch's World of Magical Foods
A Kitchen Witch's World of Magical Plants & Herbs
Arc of the Goddess (co-written with Tracey Roberts)
Moon Books Gods & Goddesses Colouring Book
(Patterson family)
Practically Pagan: An Alternative Guide to Cooking

Llewellyn

Curative Magic
A Witch for All Seasons: Spells, Rituals, Festivals, and Magic
Practical Candle Magic: Witchcraft with Wick & Wax

Solarus

Flower Magic Oracle Deck

Animal Dreaming Publishing

Magical Herbs Oracle Deck part of the Kitchen Witch series

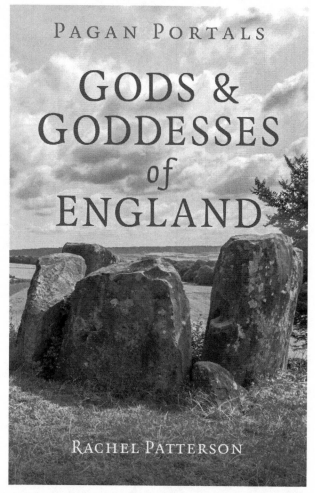

PAGAN PORTALS

GODS &
GODDESSES
of
ENGLAND

RACHEL PATTERSON

Unearthing the gods and goddesses of England, with an
aim to work and connect with these very special deities

978-1-78904-662-5 (Paperback)
978-1-78904-663-2 (e-book)

Bestsellers from Moon Books

Keeping Her Keys
An Introduction to Hekate's Modern Witchcraft
Cyndi Brannen
Blending Hekate, witchcraft and personal development
together to create a powerful new magickal perspective.
Paperback: 978-1-78904-075-3 ebook 978-1-78904-076-0

Journey to the Dark Goddess
How to Return to Your Soul
Jane Meredith
Discover the powerful secrets of the Dark Goddess and
transform your depression, grief and pain into healing
and integration.
Paperback: 978-1-84694-677-6 ebook: 978-1-78099-223-5

Shamanic Reiki
Expanded Ways of Working with Universal Life Force Energy
Llyn Roberts, Robert Levy
Shamanism and Reiki are each powerful ways of healing; together,
their power multiplies. Shamanic Reiki introduces techniques to
help healers and Reiki practitioners tap ancient healing wisdom.
Paperback: 978-1-84694-037-8 ebook: 978-1-84694-650-9

Southern Cunning
Folkloric Witchcraft in the American South
Aaron Oberon
Modern witchcraft with a Southern flair, this book is a
journey through the folklore of the American South and
a look at the power these stories hold for modern witches.
Paperback: 978-1-78904-196-5 ebook: 978-1-78904-197-2

Readers of ebooks can buy or view any of these bestsellers by clicking on the live link in the title. Most titles are published in paperback and as an ebook. Paperbacks are available in traditional bookshops. Both print and ebook formats are available online.

Find more titles and sign up to our readers' newsletter
www.collectiveinkbooks.com/paganism

For video content, author interviews and more, please subscribe to our YouTube channel.

MoonBooksPublishing

Follow us on social media for book news, promotions and more:

Facebook: Moon Books

Instagram: @MoonBooksCI

X: @MoonBooksCI

TikTok: @MoonBooksCI